The Wild Longing of the Human Heart

The Search for Happiness and Something More

William Cooney

Hamilton Books

An Imprint of
Rowman & Littlefield
Lanham • Boulder • New York • Toronto • Plymouth, UK

Preface

Brace yourself. As you read this you seem to be surrounded by relatively stable conditions of comfort and safety, but this is an illusion so hang on tight. In actuality you are on an extremely dangerous and harrowing journey, but do not feel alone because we are all in this together. The reality is that you and I are being hurled through space at roughly 67,000 miles per hour during each and every day of our lives. Each year we cover nearly 600 million miles on our trip around the Sun. All the while we are dodging dangers which could do us all in such as gamma radiation caused by exploding stars in our galaxy which may have destroyed two-thirds of all life on earth 450 million years ago, and asteroids which may have killed roughly 75% of all life forms, including the dinosaurs, some 65 million years ago.

When you consider this fact it can be dizzying and even terrifying. We rarely, if ever, consciously take notice of it. Perhaps fear prevents us from thinking of it. We often bury such things within the unconscious mind along with other fears. Sometimes avoidance brings comfort. After all our entire solar system has a grim forecast. As our Sun continues to heat up, its hydrogen core is being transformed into helium causing it to expand. In time our species will face certain death as the Sun slowly swallows its planets. Though this will not occur until billions of years into the future, still it adds to the overall dread we may face when consciously thinking of it.

Perhaps we need more time to get used to all of this. We are, after all, relative newcomers to it all. Consider this—our Sun is also engaged in a massive journey around the Milky Way galaxy itself, which has a large black hole at its center in an area named Sagittarius A. The trip takes roughly 250 million years to complete at speeds of around 600,000 mile per hour. During 99.9% of our Sun's most recent revolution around our galaxy our species did not yet even exist. Our earliest pre-hominid ancestors evolved only about two million years ago (Australopithecus, homo habilis, and homo erectus) and our modern precursors (Cro-Magnon) began to flourish only some 40–50 thousand years ago. Since then entire civilizations have come and gone, each with their own cultures, languages, religions, philosophies, arts and political systems. We know the names of some of them: Babylon, Persia, Egypt, Greece, Rome, etc. They have all risen and they have all fallen. But many societies have come and gone whose names and details are unknown to us. Recent discoveries of ruins in Gobekli Tepe near modern-day Turkey, for example, reveal a culture that thrived some 11,000–15,000 years ago with understanding of tool-making, hunting, farming, art and religion. This culture built sophisticated and complex temples 7,000 years before the Egyptian pyramids and England's Stonehenge, yet we know nothing about them.

Many more such cultures have likely come and gone throughout our world. We do not know. Yet we can be sure of this: the people living in those cultures were human and struggled each and every day of their lives to make life tolerable just like us. They worked hard to survive, they worried about their children and each other, and just like us they spent their entire lives on this terrifying journey around the sun at almost unimaginable speeds without being consciously aware of it.

But at some point, as a species and as individuals, we do need to think of it. Our journey continues to be an amazing story over eons of time: the birth of our universe 13.8 billion years ago, the formation of our Sun and of our planets some 4.5 billion years ago, the development of elements forged in those vast furnaces called stars, which eventually led to the evolution of all life on our planet as well as our species and, finally, the development of our societies.

Compared to the vast time scale of our universe, to say nothing of its unimaginable and perhaps infinite size, our individual lives are like those soap bubbles from the child's toy—they develop quickly and then evaporate in a blink of an eye. In our soap bubble lives we have so little time to learn as much as we can about our universe, about where we come from and about what lies ahead. This is why history is so important. Lessons learned and passed on by our ancestors help us all to come to terms with our past and to prepare for the present and future. Imagine if each generation had to restart it all from the beginning: the discovery of fire, agriculture, language, society, science, philosophy, art and religion, would all have to begin again over and over. History allows us to take huge leaps forwards.

In looking at our history and in taking it all in, we are all finally brought to the ultimate human question which each generation and each individual attempts to answer. This question is Alfie's question (from the book and film): "What's it all about?" As the 20th century French/Algerian existential philosopher Albert Camus once proclaimed, this is the question "why," what is behind it all, what does it all mean? Camus spoke of the "wild longing of the human heart" in search after answers to these questions. On the basic human level this amounts to the question, what is the meaning of it all, what is its goal, what is the purpose of life?

Throughout human history the most popular answer to this question has been "happiness." We say of ourselves, especially in times of struggle, that we just want to be happy. We say this of our children, too, and in the end and regardless of all else our primary and constant hope is just that we are all happy.

But what if this popular answer is wrong? What if we have missed something important? What if happiness is only part of the answer or none at all? The purpose of this book is to investigate these questions. Is happiness the answer or is there something more? What's it all about?

I

The Wild Longing of the Human Heart:
The Search for Happiness

Chapter One

The End We All Seek

What is the wild longing of the human heart? It cannot be easily explained. Perhaps it can never be fully comprehended. Nevertheless we all feel it. It is what drives us all forwards. It is the motivation for all that we feel, all that we believe, all that we love, and all that we yearn for. Aristotle once stated it clearly: "Every art and every inquiry, and similarly every action and pursuit, is thought to aim at some good; and for this reason the good has rightly been declared to be that at which all things aim."[1]

But what is this "good" he speaks of? This is the key question. Answering it requires a journey. Every journey has a beginning. So let us begin with one who took the journey. In his classic book *Walden,* Henry David Thoreau was responding to the questions why he walked away from everything and went to live alone in the woods. Why did he do this, and what was he looking for? His answer was this[2]:

> I went to the woods because I wished to live deliberately, to confront only the essential facts of life, and see if I could not learn what it had to teach, and not, when I came to die, discover that I had not lived.

Thoreau's words are where we should all begin. They are an encouragement to us to live life to its fullest. They also serve as a warning not to take the journey of life for granted. It is important to begin with Thoreau's questions. Why do we do what we do? What are we looking for? At the beginning of my classes I sometimes ask my students why they bother going to college. It's a simple question but they often look puzzled that anyone would question something so obviously good and important like higher education, especially a college professor like me. Usually I get something like "we're going to college to get a better job." But then I follow that up with "why do you want a better job?" After some befuddled looks the typical reply is "to make more

3

money." "Okay so what's the need," I ask, "for more money?" Now the stares denote a transition from confusion to irritation: everyone knows why money is valuable, right? "Well think about it," I go on, "really, why more money?" "Well," someone usually offers, "we want a better salary so that we can provide better for ourselves and our families." Fair enough. But this is not the end to the series of my questions. I go on to ask them why they want to provide for and take care of themselves and their families. This is where it starts to get interesting because someone inevitably arrives at the quintessential and seemingly all too obvious answer: "because all of us just want to be happy in life!"

However, if I am feeling daring I ask the following question: "why do you want to be happy?" This can lead to bewilderment and outright exasperation. I can understand that. In fact, as I go on to tell them, it is essentially one of the points I am trying to get at. You see there are things sought after as a means to some other end, like going to college (desired as a means to a better job) and more money (a means towards providing for oneself and family). What about happiness? Is happiness a means to something else, or is happiness the end of the series of questions? To use Aristotle's language, is happiness the "end we all seek"?

Plainly put, if something A is a means to some other end B, then it makes sense to ask: "why do you want A?" The answer will be because it will get me B. But if B is also a means to something else C, then it makes sense to ask: "why do you want B?" The answer, of course, is that it will get me C, and so on. But at some point do we reach the end of our series? Is there something Z, which is wanted for itself alone and not as a means to something else? If so, that thing Z will be what philosophers have called the *Summum Bonum* (Latin for the highest or chief good that all humans seek). It is what Aristotle calls "the good" which is "that at which all things aim." Is happiness, then, the *Summum Bonum*? In short, does happiness=Z?

Happiness does seem to be a good candidate since it appears to be less like a means and more like an end. Furthermore, there is a long-standing tradition supporting the formula: Happiness=Z. Consider the following examples:

> Happiness is the meaning and the purpose of life, the whole aim and end of human existence.—Aristotle
>
> Is not happiness precisely what all seek, so that there is not one who does not desire it?—St. Augustine
>
> All men seek happiness. This is without exception. Whatever different means they employ, they all tend to this end. The cause of some going to war, and of others avoiding it, is the same desire in both, attended with different views. This is the motive of every action of every man, even of those who hang themselves.—Blaise Pascal

The great end of all human industry is the attainment of happiness. For this were arts invented, sciences cultivated, laws ordained, and societies modeled, by the most profound wisdom of patriots and legislators. Even the lonely savage . . . forgets not, for a moment, this grand object of his being.—David Hume

The longing for happiness is never quenched in the heart of man.—Jean Jacques Rousseau

Happiness, though an indefinite concept, is the goal of all rational beings.—Immanuel Kant

Happiness is the only sanction of life; where happiness fails, existence becomes a mad lamentable experiment.—George Santayana

How to gain, how to keep, and how to recover happiness is in fact for most men at all times the secret motive for all they do.—William James

All of this seems very convincing. Happiness could indeed be the end we all seek. But besides the time-honored wisdom of these esteemed authors, what convinces us that this claim is true? Where is the evidence? Do a search among wise sources about happiness and you will find that such views are offered more in the manner of an unquestioned assumption rather than as a result of some research, investigation, or argument. No attempt to provide the evidence is made. Instead our wise sources go on to offer advice on how to achieve the end. Consider these samples:

If you want to live a happy life, tie it to a goal, not to people or things.—Albert Einstein

Nothing can bring you happiness but yourself.—Ralph Waldo Emerson

There is only one way to happiness and that is to cease worrying about things which are beyond the power of our will.—Epictetus

If you want others to be happy, practice compassion, if you want to be happy, practice compassion.—Dalai Lama

Happiness is when what you think, what you say, and what you do are in harmony.—Mahatma Gandhi

Notice that in none of the above is there the slightest attempt to provide evidence that happiness is the end we all seek. They all just assume that it is. But perhaps I am just being overly critical. Maybe the assumption about happiness is simply justified by common sense alone. If so, perhaps no real evidence is needed. John Stuart Mill stated this very case. He was a famous proponent of a theory about happiness called utilitarianism: those actions are right which promote this general principle: "the greatest happiness for the greatest number."

Mill tells us that "The utilitarian doctrine is that happiness is desirable, and the only thing desirable, as an end; all other things being only desirable as means to that end." But what proof does he offer?[3]

The only proof capable of being given that an object is visible is that people actually see it. The only proof that a sound is audible is that people hear it: . . . No reason can be given why the general happiness is desirable, except that each person, so far as he believes it to be attainable, desires his own happiness. This, however, being a fact, we have not only all the proof which the case admits of, but all which it is possible to require, that happiness is a good: that each person's happiness is a good to that person, and the general happiness, therefore, a good to the aggregate of all persons.

Maybe Mill is right. We can know that happiness is the end we all seek because everyone does, in fact, seek it. But among other things and at some point don't we need to consider what philosophers call the "is/ought" distinction? In other words, even if it appears to be the case that happiness "is" what we all or most of us seek, does it necessarily follow that happiness is what we "ought" to seek? Surely the answer is no. People often seek things they shouldn't: too much chocolate, alcohol, drugs, etc. This distinction is important and we will focus on this and similar questions later.

Another important issue, of course, is how do we define happiness? While research into happiness is replete with claims that it is the end of life and with advice on how to attain it, it falls miserably short on attempts to define it. What is happiness, anyway? What do we mean by it? Does it mean the same thing to all people and in all cultures? Are there different senses of happiness? Too often I think assumptions are made that there is no need to define it. Perhaps we think we all know what it is already and so do not even need to define it. To paraphrase the famous line from Supreme Court Justice Potter Stewart (as he and his colleagues were trying to define obscenity and pornography) "we can't define it, but we know it when we see it." But if happiness is in fact the end we all seek, might it not be worth our while to try and define it?

There often is a resistance to defining happiness. Ironically, in fact, some wise sources make the claim that trying to define or understand what happiness is may itself be a cause of unhappiness. Consider these examples:

You will never be happy if you continue to search for what happiness consists of.—Albert Camus

The search for happiness is one of the chief sources of unhappiness.—Eric Hoffer

The pursuit of happiness is a most ridiculous phrase: if you pursue happiness you'll never find it.—C.P. Snow

Happiness is a butterfly, which when pursued, is always just beyond our grasp, but which, if you will sit down quietly, may alight upon you."—Nathaniel Hawthorne

Ask yourself whether you are happy and you cease to be so.—John Stuart Mill

Maybe it's just me, but I find this more than a little dissatisfying. Surely we should be able to investigate the very nature of happiness itself. Perhaps a full definition will escape our grasp, but might we not learn something in the journey nonetheless? What is happiness, after all? What does it consist of? What are its criteria? More importantly, is happiness really the end we all seek, or is there some other end that either we do seek or ought to seek? In short, what is it all about?

Based on the title of this book, I am certain that you are able to guess that I intend to question the ancient wisdom and buck the trend. That is to say I intend to argue that in fact happiness is not and should not be the end we all seek. Perhaps this is daring. Perhaps this is foolish. You can be the judge. I will offer my arguments later. But we need to first provide closer examination of this thing called "happiness." We need to look at its history, its meaning and definition, and see what science, psychology and philosophy have learned about it. To paraphrase an idea from the 20th century philosopher Ludwig Wittgenstein, we need to climb up the ladder of happiness before we can attempt to discard it.

NOTES

1. Aristotle, Richard McKeon trans., *The Basic Works of Aristotle* (New York: Random House, 1941), Book 1, Chapter 1.
2. Henry David Thoreau, *Walden* (Boston: Ticknor and Fields, 1854), 25.
3. John Stuart Mill, *Utilitarianism* (London: Parker, Son and Bourn, 1863), Chapter 4.

Chapter Two

A Brief History of Happiness

When we look to early East Asian cultures we see differences in how happiness is conceived and achieved. In India, for example, to goal of the Hindu is to find peace and happiness through *moksha*, which refers to the escape or release from the earthly cycles of life, death and endless reincarnation. According to this view the physical world we live in is *Maya* (illusory). Real happiness is not found, then, in this world, which is in constant flux and passes away. Rather it is found only in *nirvana. Nirvana* is not a place like the Christian's heaven. Literally it refers to being extinguished like a light on a candle. This sounds odd to a Westerner. In the Hindu view of things the separate individual soul (*atman*) eventually ceases to exist as an unconnected entity when it enters the state of *nirvana. Nirvana* is experienced when the earthly soul rejoins the source of all souls, namely, the soul of God (*Brahman Atman*). Here we witness the early origins of the well-known idea from Eastern philosophy and religion: becoming one with the universe. This is the experience that Siddhartha Gautama (the Buddha) had in the 6th century BCE, while meditating under the famous *Bodhi* tree (tree of enlightenment). As a young prince Siddhartha was surrounded only by young and healthy people and sheltered from miseries like sickness and old age. This reveals his Hindu upbringing—though old age is respected and honored, it is not directly the goal of the seeker of true happiness in India. The goal is to be released (*moksha*) from this material realm and from the enduring miseries of the wheel or rebirth (*samsara*).[1]

The goal of the Taoist in China, on the other hand, is in many respects just the opposite of the Hindu. The point is to endure and live as long as possible here in the earthly realm, not to escape it. One of the reasons the tortoise is an object of worship in ancient China is because it is a creature that has learned to live to a ripe old age. The *Tao* is the Way or Path of the universe. The *Tao*

9

is what must be imitated as an attempt to extend our lives. In this way the microcosm (small universe) imitates the macrocosm (large universe), namely, by finding happiness in peace, naturalness, and spontaneity, as described by the sage Lao Tzu in the *Tao Te Ching* in the 6th century BCE. Another strong influence on ancient China comes about a half-century later from Kung Fu Tzu (Confucius) who saw happiness not so much as an individual accomplishment, but as the result of a well-ordered family and social life. For Confucius the key Chinese word is not *tao*, but *li*, which refers to proper social actions and relationships. Happiness is not found, he taught, in looking to the heavens like the Taoists encouraged, rather it is found in our earthly and social interactions; child to parent, citizen to country, nation to the larger world. [2]

But while the paths to happiness may differ in cultures, the notion of happiness itself as a subjective state or feeling of contentment and/or joy in response to good circumstances or good fortune seems to be generally cross-cultural. The Japanese word for happiness, for example, is *kofuku*, which comes from the combination of *ko* (lucky) and *fuku* (fortune). Likewise the Persian word is *khushi* (also used in Urdo and Hindi languages), signifying a comfortable life of good fortune. This is the root for the English word "cushion" and has led to the phrase a "cushy life." The Chinese have a number of words signifying happiness according to different degrees. The highest is *xingfu*, meaning a long-lasting and blessed life. In African languages the word for happiness also means joy (e.g., the Swahili *furaha*, and the Zulu *injabulo*). The concepts expressed in all of these terms from foreign lands and tongues, then, would be recognizable to any Westerner. [3]

This should not be all that surprising. It is reasonable to believe that happiness is felt in a similar way throughout all cultures, since it is so universally expressed in a similar way in the faces of each and every one of us, namely, in the way we smile. As reported in Stefan Klein's book, *The Science of Happiness*, the smile is now known to be universal. As Klein details it, researcher Paul Eckman set on the path of this discovery. One context is a theory of learned behavior known as the "blank slate theory." This is the view that babies enter into the world as a *tabula rasa* (an empty tablet). Aristotle was the originator of this view 2,300 years ago with his famous words: "the mind at birth is like a writing tablet upon which nothing stands written." [4] According to this theory, the smile would have to be learned behavior just like everything else. But it would be difficult to explain how the smile could be so universal. Eckman found that the expression of the genuine smile, which he named the "Duchenne smile" [5] (after the scientist who first studied the muscles surrounding the eye), is found throughout the world. To paraphrase the old Jimmy Durante song "the whole world smiles like you." In the Duchenne smile the corners of the mouth go up along with a narrowing of the eyes. In fact, as Klein reports, even children blind from birth will respond with this kind of smile to moments of joy and happiness. In this case, as least, it seems that the blank slate theory is wrong. Babies enter the world already knowing how to do something: they are born knowing how to smile.

When we do an etymology (study of root meanings of words) of the English word "happiness,"[6] some interesting things turn up. As early as the 1200s happiness was used to reflect an element of good luck, similar to the notion of non-Western cultures, as we have seen. There is a connection to Old English from an Old Germanic word "*happ*" meaning chance or good fortune. This notion is still reflected in such words as "happenstance." By the 1500s happiness was used to mean "good fortune" and this notion ties in well with other Western languages: the Latin *felicitas* (happy, fortunate), the French *bonheur* (good fortune), and the German *glück* (luckiness). It is note-worthy that something like the opposite of happiness has related words as well. The word "disaster," for instance, comes from the Latin for ill or diseased star (seen as the sign of ill, rather than good, fortune). So in the very words used for happiness there seem to be two elements: an event or incident of good fortune, followed by a feeling of contentment or joy. In all this there is the recognition that happiness is tied to what happens to us (stimulus), and the attendant feeling we have (response).

When we do a historical survey of the concept of happiness in the West beginning in ancient Greece, the cradle of Western civilization, we find that the hedonist philosophers claimed that happiness is a kind of pleasure (*he-done*). But what kind of pleasure is happiness? There were two overall schools of thought on this point. In the 4th century BCE Aristippus and others taught that the pleasures we should seek are the physical ones produced in experiencing the best foods, wines, and other sensual satisfactions including sex. As the first century Christian missionary St. Paul was later to claim, this is the philosophy of "eat, drink and be merry, for tomorrow we may die."[7] A century after Aristippus, Epicurus argued that this is a philosophy "fit for swine."[8] He offered a new form of hedonism arguing that we humans have higher and more elevated faculties than mere swine; in particular we have minds. The pleasure he encouraged was *ataraxia.* This sounds like either a disease or an eighties heavy metal band. If after a physical your doctor told you that you have *ataraxia*, you'd most likely ask for a shot of antibiotics. However, *ataraxia* refers to something good. From the Greek it means tran-quility or peace of mind. For Epicurus this mental or psychological pleasure can be attained by removing fears and anxieties from our minds, most not-ably the fears related to death.

For both types of hedonism happiness is seen as a feeling, either physical or mental. Not all ancient philosophers saw happiness as a feeling, however. Long before the hedonists, Plato described *eudaimonia* as the goal. This Greek word is usually translated in English as "happiness" but it deserves a far richer meaning, which we shall discuss later. For Plato *eudaimonia* is achieved through a harmony or balance of the disparate elements of the *psyche* (mind). Plato offered a tripartite theory of the mind: the rational (headed up by the reason and logic) and the non-rational (comprised of the spirited element or the conscience, and the appetites which seek satisfaction of selfish needs). These ideas were forerunners to Sigmund Freud's id, super-ego, and ego developed some 2300 years later. For both Freud and Plato, happiness can only be achieved in a proper harmonization of the disparate elements of the mind.

Plato's brilliant student Aristotle discussed happiness at more length. He was convinced that all humans seek it as an end. He was equally convinced that most never achieve it because we often make mistakes in pursuing it. On the one hand we seek it in the wrong place: e.g., money, power, popularity. On the other hand we have a wrong idea about what happiness is in the first place. For Aristotle happiness is not a feeling at all. Most people think of happiness as *euphoria* (good feeling), but Aristotle teaches us that this is a mistake. He agreed with Plato that happiness is *eudaimonia,* not *euphoria.* The Greek *eudaimonia* is a word arrived at by the combination of the prefix *eu* (good) with *daimon* (spirit or character). This notion of happiness, then, suggests a state of good or virtuous character: it is a state of being not a feeling. Aristotle's famous definition of happiness as *eudaimonia* is "activity of soul in accordance with virtue."[9] This idea is plainly alien to us now because the long tradition of happiness as a feeling has made its mark. Though, as we shall see, many contemporary psychologists are now using Aristotle's *eudaimonia* as a better understanding of what happiness is or should be and many use it synonymously with concepts such as "well being" or human "flourishing."

There are still other views on happiness from the ancient world. The Stoics saw happiness as *apatheia*, the source of our word "apathy," though in its original meaning it did not carry the negative connotation of simply not caring about anything. *Apatheia* is not so much a feeling as it is a psychological acceptance that things in life are outside of our control. The first century Roman Stoic philosopher Epictetus famously argued that "we are all actors in a play" and we must come to terms with the fact that we cannot change what happens in our world, we can only change our attitude towards what happens.[10] The attitude recommended is *apatheia,* which is a non-emotional acceptance of the way things are. According to their philosophy this acceptance is the only logical choice we have. The Stoics believed in a force in the universe that was in charge of all things and determined all things to be the way they are. They called this force *"Logos"* (Reason). Reason is in charge, not us. The way to be happy, then, is to align our attitudes (the only thing we can control) with things as they happen (which is out of our control, since all things are caused to happen by Logos/Reason). And if we do not understand why miseries visit us in life, we need only remember that Reason is in charge and knows best. Here lies the origin of the well-known and well-worn phrase: "There is a reason for everything."

The Stoic view of happiness was popular in the Roman period and had many famous proponents. None was more prominent than 2nd century Emperor Marcus Aurelius. His famous *Meditations*, among other things, express the stoic philosophy of happiness. He had a brilliant mind but apparently was not always considerate of the happiness of others. He was especially unkind to the Christians whom he saw as dangerous since their theology included the notion that we can in fact change what happens and also that happiness can only be found in a world beyond this present life. Like some Roman emperors before him, Marcus Aurelius actively passed laws against the Christians and openly supported their persecution and even their execution. But Christianity was to have its revenge. It began to have a foothold in Rome chiefly through the efforts of the emperor Constantine in the 4th century, who converted to the faith and eventually Christianity was declared the official religion of the Roman Empire, the most powerful political force on earth at the time, in 380. This was quite a success story for Christianity which was considered in its first few centuries to be a simply a nuisance and, later, a dangerous cult.

Under Christian influences a new view of happiness emerged. People were no longer to look for happiness on earth, but rather to bare the trials and tribulations of the here and now in hopes of achieving happiness in an afterlife. Human beings were tainted, after all, by the original sin of Adam and Eve in the paradise of the Garden of Eden. Because of this "fall" we were considered wretched and in need of salvation. Things like poverty and suffering became Christian virtues. Asceticism, or a life deprived of the physical pleasures or earthly comforts and happiness, became the ideal. John the Baptist, after all, wore chaffing garments and survived living in the desert on locust and honey. This was not a life for whiners and slackers.

In the Christian vision the only experience of happiness in the earthly realm is found in catching a temporary glimpse of the divine. This is best described by St. Augustine in the 5th century, with his notion of happiness as *beatitudo* (beatitude). The ultimate end of all humans on this earth, he taught, was a beatific vision wherein the soul can look upon God as the ultimate source of happiness. In the 13th century the Christian intellectual giant St. Thomas Aquinas, agreed with this idea. Beatitude can be achieved only partially here on earth, he argued, since the ultimate destination for humans is only found completely and perfectly in an afterlife. This was available, of course, only to the most faithful. The rest of the world was covered in a sort of dark ages for happiness, known as the medieval period (Middle Ages), for a thousand years (roughly the 4th through the 14th centuries). It is not as if seeking an earthly happiness became illegal, mind you, although it might have been fun to be charged with such a crime. Certainly common citizens found some joy in an average day let us hope, at least. Nevertheless an earthly happiness was not openly supported by the Church, which was, after all, the chief institution providing guidance to the lives of people.

Although a work of fiction, the brilliant novel by Italian scholar Umberto Eco, *The Name of the Rose*, accurately portrays the attitude of the Church towards the pursuit of what it deemed folly and frivolous, namely, such things as happiness and joy. The story centers around a lost work of Aristotle's written on a very delightful form of happiness, i.e., comedy. And what, pray tell, is so wrong with comedy? The Church's attitude is represented in a key line delivered by one of the dogmatic faithful who condemns comedy in the following way: "Laughter kills fear, and without fear there can be no faith, because without fear of the Devil there is no more need of God."[11]

The Church openly discouraged an earthly pursuit of happiness and even punished it during the worst of times. During the infamous Inquisition against unbelievers and protestors, which was all too real, the Church delivered an attack on freedom of thought (which many would deem an important ingredient in happiness), torturing to death any who would dare to disagree with its main beliefs.

During the Renaissance in Europe (14th through to the 17th century), people began to break away from Medieval views concerning life and happiness. New worlds had been opened up and new human beings had been discovered on the other side of this round earth that seemed to live in a relatively happy coexistence with their world. There were new worlds available in new technologies developed by the sciences as well. The microscope, for example, gave us a glimpse into the micro-universe existing in a drop of water, and the telescope extended our vision into the macro-universe in all of its immense glory. The printing press, too, may be the most important invention of all since it greatly expanded knowledge. People could learn to read for themselves and in their own languages. Consequently they became less dependent on the Church and clerics for information, even about theological and scriptural matters. This threatened the power and control of the Church and was a main reason why it condemned the translation of the Bible into foreign languages. From the 4th century the Church declared that the only valid translation of the Bible was the Latin *Vulgate,* which was translated from Aramaic, Hebrew, and Greek by St. Jerome. The thought that the Holy Book would be translated into common languages beginning in the 14th-16th centuries, such as English (accomplished by John Wycliffe), French (by Jacques Lefevre d'Etaples) and German (by Martin Luther) terrified the Church. After all, why would you need to consult the Church or the local priest about what the Holy Book said if you could read it for yourself? The printing press allowed people to cut out the middleman!

The great advances in medicine during the Renaissance also offered hope for the cure of common illnesses and an extension of life. All of this seemed very hopeful and the future of human wellbeing and happiness seemed bright. Happiness, or at least the hope for it, seemed to break free from the dark ages of the Medieval period. People began to openly disagree with the dealings of the Church and its controls on everyday thought and life. More directly, they began to attack the Church's behavior. The Church, they felt, focused too much on the afterlife and too easily justified its own cruel behaviors here on earth. Montaigne stated it most eloquently: "I have always observed a singular accord between supercelestial ideas and subterranean behavior."[12] Dante placed seven popes in Hell in his classic work, *The Divine Comedy*. Erasmus contributed to the on-going criticism with his books *Julius Exclusus* (wherein Pope Julius is not allowed entrance into heaven) and *In Praise of Folly* (a thorough criticism of the Church's behavior which played an important role in the Protestant Reformation). Later, Michelangelo placed Pope Julius in hell in his famous *Last Judgment* scene on the altar wall of the Sistine Chapel. All of this must've provided sweet revenge, at least in fantasy, to those poor souls whose search for simple happiness was dashed on a daily basis by the ominous presence the Church had on their lives.

By the time of the Enlightenment or what's called the "Age of Reason" in France (late 17th and 18th centuries), there was an optimistic attitude about finding happiness and a focus on personal development of the individual. The critique of the Church continued. In the *Encyclopédie*, which contained the key philosophical writings of philosophers such as Diderot and Voltaire, we find the essential claim from the Age of Reason: "Reason is to the philosopher what grace is to the Christian."[13] The intent is clear: reason and science will replace faith and religion and help deliver the human race out of the life of poverty, suffering and disease. This can be done, argued Voltaire, when we realize that "the only antidote to suffering and despair is to work to cultivate the human garden."[14] This included social reforms as well as the rejection of intolerance from the Church or other authorities, and a focus on freedoms in thought, speech, and religion. One of Voltaire's most famous lines derides the intolerance in previous centuries: "I may not agree with what you have to say, but I'll defend to the death your right to say it." [15] And so the focus on the right to freedom of thought and expression became cornerstones of a new found promise of happiness.

Voltaire's countryman Jean Jacques Rousseau also provided a critique of the Church's view of human nature. In particular he criticized the notion of original sin by declaring that "there is no original perversity in the human heart."[16] Rousseau more fully developed the notion of happiness as tied to the celebration of one's individuality as opposed to following the crowd or "herd." "Dare to be yourselves," he argued, since trying to copy everyone else will lead to inauthentic existence and unhappiness. His ideas helped to usher in a new period in history known as Romanticism, which along with individualism, emphasized the role of feelings which are according to Rousseau "the first impulses of nature" and "always right." This can be seen as the origin of many modern sentiments: be yourself, follow your true feelings, follow your heart, listen to your gut, etc. The 19th century British Romantic writers Wordsworth, Coleridge, Shelly, and Keats, were inspired to explore these and other ideas in their poetry.

Rousseau also helped to foster the notion of human rights in France. To that extent he contributed to the famous outcry of the French Revolution "liberty, equality, fraternity." Napoleon claimed the revolution would not have happened without the contributions of Rousseau, his favorite author. Three quarters of a century before Rousseau, John Locke championed human rights in England and likewise his ideas helped to inspire the British Revolution. The tie-in to happiness was clear. Locke, after all, is one of the fathers of the phrase "the right to pursue happiness,"[17] those famous words that helped to inspire a country born from their spirit: the United States of America. Locke also postulated the "right to private property," an important ingredient to a capitalistic economic system. The 18th century Scottish philosopher and father of economics Adam Smith also argued for a *laissez-faire* (hands-off) government so that a free market can allow for the natural forces of supply and demand, ensuring the happiness of both consumers and businesses.

The 19th century brought a full-fledged capitalism into the world. There was the promise of a greater happiness born of greater prosperity. But as the classes of rich and poor began to divide more clearly, philosopher and father of socialism/communism Karl Marx rejected this as a false or "*bourgeois*" (ownership class) happiness. Rather than happiness, he argued, what capitalism brings is a special type of unhappiness that he expressed in German as "*entfremdung*" (estrangement or alienation). This consisted of a deep psychological and physical separation from our true human needs, created by a division of people into unequal classes. The Marxist solution was the elimination of these classes by dispensing with the right to private property. You cannot have an ownership/*bourgeois* class (the "haves" which leave out the "have-nots") if nothing can be owned. The core ideas of Marx were neatly summed up in his famous call: "to each according to their needs, from each according to their abilities."[18] This meant that the benefits of society (those things we need for basic happiness: food, shelter, transportation, schools, etc.) should be given out equally, since humans have basically equal needs. But then what would be the incentive to be a brain surgeon, for example, which requires so much more work than being, say, a gardener, if both brain surgeon and gardener receive the same basic goods? The Marxist answer seems to be that the desire to serve the overall good of the State, as opposed to satisfying one's own selfish desires, would be enough. Is it? There is also a further problem. Under the Marxist vision of society whether you become a brain surgeon or a gardener is based on your abilities (supposedly determined by the State) not on your free choices. Individual freedoms seem to go out the window.

The loss of freedom, as we have already seen, seems to be an essential loss in happiness as well. And the Industrial Revolution was all too powerful to be stopped by the battle cry of Marx: "Workers of the World Unite!"[19] By the turn of the 20th century in America, the engine of capitalism had a full head of steam. It was the dawning of a new age for personal and individual happiness: the promise of food on every plate, a car in every driveway, and a safe and secure roof over every head, in short, the promise of the good life.

How has America fared on this promise? Looking back over time with the advantage of 20/20 hindsight, we can try to draw some conclusions based in the research. Sometimes it's a mixed bag. A study reported in the journal *ScienceDaily*[20] suggests, not surprisingly, that people in America are happiest depending on the quality of life in their State. But lest we become too content with this seemingly obvious fact, the same journal reports[21] that suicide rates are highest in those States rated happiest! Go figure. What about the question: "can money buy happiness?" Klein reports research that shows that the richest 50 Americans are only slightly happier than Americans with average incomes. Some have offered a theory about this. Evidence reported in *Scientific American*[22] suggests that wealthier people are less happy because they become less appreciative of the everyday small pleasures in life. In any case happiness does not seem necessarily tied to one's wealth status, and a study detailed in *Time*[23] suggests a "paradox in American happiness" in that during times of economic downturn, people report being happier and more optimistic about the future. What is more, Nobel prize-winning psychologist Daniel Kahneman reports a study that shows that Americans with $60,000 household incomes are as measurably happy as billionaires![24]

And how does America compare with other nations? A report by the OECD (Organization for Economic Cooperation and Development) listed America as ranking as high as 12th and as low as 19th, depending on the measure used. It listed Denmark as the happiest country among those studied.[25] A study reviewed in *Forbes* lists America slightly higher at number 10.[26] In recent data from the *World Happiness Report*,[27] the United States finished 15th, while the top ten countries were mostly European in this order: Switzerland (as noted by the author of the report, this is the one that consumes the most chocolate!), Iceland (apparently colder climates can still produce smiles), Denmark, Norway, Canada, Finland, The Netherlands, Sweden, New Zealand and Australia.

Measuring happiness is not an exact science and it greatly depends on the criteria used. The *World Happiness Study* used six factors: income per capita, low crime and corruption, generosity, social support, individual freedoms and physical and mental health. Statistical information from self-reported life satisfaction studies often use economic indicators such as low unemployment, availability of schools, hospitals, museums, parks, and other amenities. But these statistics can be highlighted for good results, or traded for others to embellish them. As Mark Twain once remarked, "There are three kinds of lies: lies, damned lies, and statistics."[28] There is also the problem of self-reporting. We can ask people how happy they are and ask them even to attach some quantitative description (on a scale of 1 to 10), but we can never be completely sure how reliable this is. Their perception is not always reality. Kahneman has also explained and examined the difference between two kinds of selves: the "remembering self" and the "experiencing self."[29] The actual pleasure and/or pain experienced by the self, he shows, is different from what the self remembers. The "remembering self," he says, is a story-teller and seemingly biased by the goals of the story it tries to reconstruct.

While there may be no completely convincing and measurable leap in the experience of happiness in America or in other parts of the world, there certainly has been an explosion of information about happiness beginning in the late 20th and early 21st centuries. In large part this can be attributed to two areas: a deeper understand of happiness as it comes from the sciences (brain research, in particular), and the development of Positive Psychology. It is to these subjects we shall now turn.

NOTES

1. For an overview of Hinduism and Buddhism see David S. Noss and Blake R. Grangaard, *History of the World's Religions* (New York: Pearson Publishing, 2012), Chapters 4 and 6.

2. For an overview of Taoism and Confucianism see Noss and Grangaard, Chapter 8.

3. The foreign words for happiness are retrieved from the website below, last retrieved on 9/10/15: http://en.organisasi.org/translation/happiness-in-other-languages.

4. Aristotle, *De Anima*, Richard McKeon, trans., *The Basic Works of Aristotle,* (New York: Random House, 1941), 429b-430a.

5. Stefan Klein, *The Science of Happiness: How Our Brains Make Us Happy—and What We Can Do to Get Happier* (New York: Marlowe and Company, 2006), 8–9.

6. See Etymology Dictionary Online at http://etymonline.com/.

7. St. Paul. *First Corinthians*,15:32. New Testament, NIV.

8. For an overview of Epicurus see the entry "Epicurus," from the *Stanford Encyclopedia of Philosophy*: http://epicurus.stanford.edu/entire/epicurus/.

9. Aristotle, *Nicomachean Ethics*, in Richard McKeon, trans., *The Basic Works of Aristotle* (New York: Random House, 1941), 1098a.

10. Epictetus, Discourses and Selected Writings, Robert Dobbin, trans. (London: Penguin Classics, 2008), Chapter 17.

11. Umberto Ecco, *The Name of the Rose* (New York: Harcourt, 1983). This quotation is also found on 9/10/15 at http://www.plentyquotes.com/movies/The-Name-of-the-Rose/The-Name-of-the-Rose-3.html.

12. Michel deMontaigne, *"Of Experience,"* Charles Cotton, trans., (Paris, 1588), 65.

13. Denis Diderot and Voltaire, *Encyclopédie* (Paris: Andre le Breton Publisher, 1751–1772).

14. For Voltaire's quote see the information from the following website, retrieved on 9/10/15: http://www.quotationspage.com/quote/331.html.

15. For Voltaire's quote see the following website last accessed on 9/10/15: http://www.quotationspage.com/quote/331.html.

16. Jean Jacques Rousseau, *Emile: Treatise on Education*, (Paris: 1762), Book One.

17. For a discussion of Locke's phrase see this website, last accessed on 9/10/15: http://www.pursuit-of-happiness.org/history-of-happiness/john-locke/.

18. Karl Marx, "Critique of the Gotha Program." (1875) Part One.

19. Karl Marx and Friedrich Engels, *The Communist Manifesto*, (United Kingdom, 1848).

20. ScienceDaily article, retrieved on 9/10/15 from: http://www.sciencedaily.com/releases/2009/12/091217141314.htm.

21. ScienceDaily article, retrieved on 9/10/15 from: http://www.sciencedaily.com/releases/2011/04/110421082641.htm.

22. Scientific American article, retrieved on 9/10/15 from: http://www.scientificamerican.com/article.cfm?id=can-money-buy-happiness

23. Time Magazine, "The Happiness Paradox," retrieved on 9/10/15 from: http://www.time.com/time/magazine/article/0,9171,1938719,00.html

24. Daniel Kahneman, *Thinking: Fast and Slow* (New York: Farrar, Straus and Giroux, 2011).

25. OECD Report retrieved on 9/10/15 from: http://www.lifeslittlemysteries.com/denmark-happiest-country-2088/.

26. Forbes Magazine Study retrieved on 9/10/15 from: http://www.forbes.com/2011/01/19/norway-denmark-finland-business-washington-world-happiest-countries_2.html.

27. "Report on World Happiness" (4/24/15) retrieved on 9/10/15 from: https://www.yahoo.com/health/the-10-happiest-countries-on-earth-117266806377.html.

28. For Mark Twain's quote, see the following website last retrieved on 9/10/15: http://www.twainquotes.com/Statistics.html.

29. Daniel Kahneman: TED lecture (2009), "The Remembering Self," retrieved on 9/10/15 from: http://www.ted.com/talks/daniel_kahneman_the_riddle_of_experience_vs_memory

Chapter Three

Happiness and the Brain

Each of us has a universe inside our heads. As reported by neuroscientists the brain is comprised of approximately 1 trillion cells and 100 billion neurons, making a possible combination of practically limitless brain states equaling 10 to the millionth power.[1] This number is said to be larger than the number of atoms that exist in the entire known universe, which is estimated to be 10 to the 80th power! Consider the immensity of the task, then, as we set out trying to understand the human brain (the inner universe). By comparison after many centuries we are only beginning to understand the physical world (the outer universe). A little more than four centuries ago—a millisecond of time on the evolutionary scale—we believed that the whole universe was made up only of our solar system, and that our earth was positioned at the center of it all (this was called the geocentric theory; *geo*=earth in Greek). Now we know that Copernicus and Galileo were right in proposing the sun-centered view (this was called the heliocentric theory; *helios*=sun in Greek) and modern science tells us that our solar system is just one of countless systems within the Milky Way galaxy which has another 200 billion suns in it, numbering like the grains of sand on all of the beaches on earth. The Milky Way galaxy, too, is just one in a seeming infinite sea of galaxies. Our universe is much larger than we can even imagine.

The Greeks called the universe the *cosmos* (meaning order). They believed, that is, that the universe is an orderly and rational place that could be understood with the use of *logos* (logic and reason). Fittingly the branch of physics studying the universe is called "cosmology" (*cosmos* + *logos*). But however orderly and rational the physical universe may be, the universe within is not entirely rational. The brain, we know, is an organ of both rational and non-rational make-up. Nobel prize winning psychologist Daniel Kahneman discusses this in his book *Thinking: Fast and Slow* wherein he outlines two types of thinking he calls "system1" or "fast thinking" and "system 2" or "slow thinking."[2] Fast thinking is emotional, intuitive, and non-rational. As Kahneman argues, fast thinking includes "innate skills that we share with other animals. We are born prepared to perceive the world around us, recognize objects, orient attention, avoid losses, and fear spiders." Slow thinking, on the other hand, is rational, demonstrative and deliberate. It is, he says, "the conscious, reasoning self that has beliefs, makes choices, and decides what to think about and what to do."[3] Sometimes, of course, the mind can be in conflict given these opposing rational and non-rational forces.

This is not a new idea. As we have seen Plato proposed a similar notion in the 4th century BCE by suggesting that the mind/*psyche* is divided into both the rational (the reason) and the non-rational (the spirited element or con-science, and the appetitive desires of the mind), leaving us with a tripartite mind. Some 2,300 years after Plato Sigmund Freud gave us his famous trinity as well: ego (the conscious and rational mind); superego (the con-science); and the id (the unconscious mind driven by desire). Incidentally, for both Plato and Freud true happiness is found in a healthy mind that balances these rational and non-rational forces, with reason at the helm and in control.

Plato illustrated this in his *Phaedrus* where he likened the mind to a charioteer (representing reason) keeping two horses under his control. The stronger unruly horse (representing the unconscious and non-rational desire or the appetite) makes the ride more difficult, since it does not easily listen to reason. Fortunately there is a nobler horse (representing the spirit and moral conscience), which is a natural ally of the rational soul and helps the chariot-eer keep the horse of desire in check.[4]

When Plato proposed this idea so many centuries ago he could not possibly have realized how close his ideas would be to our modern understanding of the brain. The neuroscientist Dr. Paul Maclean, for example, discussed the triune brain in the late 1960s. His theory has been widely accepted as an advance in our understanding of how the brain evolved in order to handle the emotions. In 1990 he elaborated on this in his book *The Triune Brain in Evolution*.[5] According to this view, inside each and every one of us is a brain divided into three parts (just as Plato had theorized): the Brain Stem (Reptil-ian brain—seat of basic emotions such as fear and aggression, but also ex-citements and pleasures, etc.); the Limbic System (Mammalian brain—seat of more complex emotions, care for the young, attachment to a partner and/or group, etc.); and finally the Cerebral cortex (Human brain—seat of reason and logic, and an ability to understand and control the emotions).

Adding to this complexity there are also voluntary and non-voluntary/automatic parts at work in the nervous system to which the brain is tied. As Klein discusses, there are two different kinds of systems operating within each of us: the VNS (voluntary nervous system, issuing from the cerebral cortex) and the ANS (autonomic nervous system, which begins in the brain stem). The VNS, he writes, is in touch with "our wishes, imaginations and thoughts." It is called "voluntary" because within it there are rational controls and choices available to us. The ANS, on the other hand and as Klein states it, is in touch with "unconscious movements of the body (heartbeat, circulation, perspiration) and causes us to blush when we're embarrassed, our hair to stand on end when we're afraid, and our pulse to race when we're in love."[6] The ANS is neither voluntary nor rational. Klein concludes, "Since, as its name suggests, we have no control over the autonomic system, we can't simply decide to be happy."[7]

Klein's point is extremely important for us to understand. A happy life is a delicate dance between the rational and non-rational, the voluntary and involuntary, and the conscious and unconscious forces within us all. Too often we are insensitive to this reality. For example we too easily blame people (or ourselves) for suffering things such as depression, as if it was simply a matter of choice. We tell someone (or ourselves) in this condition, for instance, to "snap out of it" or "stop being so negative about life," when in fact things are far more complicated than this and science can help us all to be more understanding of the fact that we are all somewhat at the mercy of forces outside our control.

Understanding the brain can help us to avoid this kind of insensitivity. We are not all the way there yet, but we are making remarkable strides. There have been many interesting discoveries as reported in Klein and elsewhere. To begin with we have developed imaging technology that allows us to actually see what the brain is doing when we are happy or feel joy. This can allow us to better target and attempt to understand those parts of the brain involved in positive feelings. We have learned that the brain has what Klein calls a "happiness system" or a "special circuitry for joy, pleasure and euphoria." It is reasonable to suppose, therefore, as Klein does, "that happiness is part of the natural, healthy, functioning of the brain."[8] In other related research, neuroscientist Christopher deCharms tells us of the brain's own powers to heal itself. During MRIs a patient can watch their own brain processes and select areas related to pain and learn how to control it. This can be done, he argues, by enabling the brain to release its own endogenous opiates to alleviate the pain.[9]

There's also more good news. Science is showing us that the brain is a malleable organ and continues to change, as we grow older: this is known as "neuroplasticity." This means that we can be positive about the fact that we can grow our ability to feel happiness, and that an "old dog" can, in fact, "learn new tricks." So although we are subject to some forces outside our control, we are not simply passive victims. We can actively participate in our own happiness.

This means, incidentally, that the ancient Greek philosophers were right: happiness is not something that simply happens to us as we passively and helplessly wait for it. We have to seek it out in activity, which can reprogram the brain towards happiness. This compares well to Aristotle's definition noted earlier: "Happiness is *activity* of soul."

Martin Seligman (the founder of positive psychology which we will discuss in the next chapter) and others point out that happiness seems to be partly tied to biology, while the rest seems tied to life circumstances and the kinds of choices we make in the face of these. People with an inherited biochemistry for depression, for example, and who also suffer a horrible fate (the death of a young child, for instance) are not prisoners of these conditions. They can make affirmative life choices in the face of these difficulties and find happiness in their lives. This is highlighted by other psychologists such as Jonathan Haidt in his book *The Happiness Hypothesis,* where he recounts the famous "happiness formula" cited by Seligman and many others in this field. [10] This formula is presented as H=S+C+V: Happiness (H) is tied to one's biological set point (S) and the overall circumstances and conditions of our lives (C), along with the voluntary choices we make and the activities we pursue (V). Most researchers believe that our set point is 50% or more of the equation. And while life's circumstances are not totally in our control, these can be balanced by our free decisions and actions.

And as Klein and others report we are also gaining a better understanding of the role certain neurotransmitters play in happiness: e.g., dopamine, oxytocin, and beta-endorphins, which help to bring about positive feelings and desires. We are learning that the opposite of happiness too, such as fear and sadness, are also linked with acetlycholine and cortisol (a stress hormone).

We are also learning that the right and left hemispheres of the brain play important roles. Klein and others report that the left side seems to be the source of more positive feelings like optimism, and damage to it can lead to sadness and depression. Damage to the right side, on the other hand, can lead to cheerfulness. Interestingly, as Klein reports, a "genuine smile, as Paul Ekman discovered, also coincides with a noticeable intensification of activity in the prefrontal cortex's left half." [11]

Much more needs to be researched and understood, but given that the right side is linked to artistic and creative thought, perhaps this can help us understand why so many famous artistic people (e.g., Vincent Van Gogh, Ernest Hemmingway and Emily Dickinson) had such tortured psyches and why some, unfortunately, took the ultimate end through suicide.

But lest we become too comfortable with this left/right distinction, a notable counter-example is found in the case of Dr. Jill Bolte. During 1996 Bolte (a Harvard brain scientist) suffered a massive stroke in the left hemisphere resulting in dependence on the right hemisphere. She reports a deep feeling of euphoria and a "sense of connection with the universe" which she describes as "Nirvana" and which she had not experienced before the illness, as a left-brained scientist. [12]

Much other related brain research continues to fascinate. Consider love, for example, which can be considered a very treasured and special kind of happiness. Anthropologist Helen Fisher and her neuroscientist colleague Lucy Brown discuss where love is located in the brain. It resides in the midbrain near the base, in the VTA (ventral tegmental area) that manufactures dopamine. Ironically, this is the same area of the brain associated with addictions, and certainly there are examples when love seems to be a kind of addiction.

Looked at from the Platonic/Macleanean perspective of the triune brain, love lives below the rational and cognitive level, in the reptilian core of the brain. This gives deeper meaning to the well-known and often cited phrase from Shakespeare that "love is blind," and the common notion that "love is not rational." As Fisher herself indicates, "love lies below the cognitive layer of the brain." Fisher's other research provides evidence for three main drives supported by brain systems (all of them related to kinds of happiness): lust or the sex drive, the aforementioned romantic love, and finally, attachment. In the end, however, she argues that happiness may not be in the cards for us all. "We are not an animal built to be happy," she says, rather, "we were built to reproduce."[13]

Sex, love and attachment, it seems, are all part of the other-directedness of our species—i.e., we need each other; we are social creatures. Empathy plays an important role in this and provides the pathway to build bridges between us and contributes, therefore, to the overall happiness of individuals and society. Neurologist Vilayanur Ramachandran explores how empathy is based in the brain. He speaks of "mirror neurons" discovered in the 1980s and 90s by neuroscientist Giacomo Rizzolatti and his colleagues at the University of Parma, Italy. These neurons reside in the front of the brain and evolved roughly 100 thousand years ago. They seem to mimic or mirror the actual feelings that others may be experiencing and help us to adopt the other's point of view. Ramachandran believes that these neurons enable us to create social bonds, societies and civilization itself. Through mirror neurons, he argues, we literally feel the feelings of others:[14]

> So, I call them Gandhi neurons, or empathy neurons. And this is not some abstract metaphorical sense. All that's separating you from him, from the other person, is your skin. Remove the skin, and you experience that person's touch in your mind. You've dissolved the barrier between you and other human beings. And this, of course, is the basis of much of Eastern philosophy, and that is there is no real independent self, aloof from other human beings, inspecting the world, inspecting other people. You are, in fact, connected not just via Facebook and the Internet, you are actually quite literally connected by your neurons. And there is a whole chain of neurons around this room, talking to each other. And there is no real distinctness of your consciousness from

somebody else's consciousness. And this is not mumbo-jumbo philosophy. It
emerges from our understanding of basic neuroscience.

This idea is very intriguing. A similar notion of interconnection is seen in
the work of cognitive scientist Douglas Hofstadter. In his classic work *Gödel
Escher Bach* and his follow-up book *I am a Strange Loop*, he proposes the
idea that each human mind is not limited to one brain, but distributed over
numerous brains. By analogy he attempts to understand the mind by comparing it to the social organization of a colony of ants, each working independently, though guided by common goals to act in concert. Taking this idea to
its logical conclusion, he argues "that by gradually widening the scope of the
brain/Mind system, one will in the end come to a feeling of being at one with
the entire universe."[15]

As Ramachandran stated, this idea squares with the thoughts of much
Eastern religion and philosophy. But it is also consistent with at least one
interpretation of Aristotle's view of the mind as well. Specifically, Aristotle
spoke of an "agent intellect," which some scholars interpret as something
like a divine or world mind that we all participate in with our individual
minds.[16] Another theory of interconnection as well, can be found in the work
of famed psychologist and successor to Freud, Carl Jung, in particular his
theory of the "collective unconsciousness" which, he claimed, we all can tap
into and participate in.[17]

We began this chapter by comparing the mind and the universe. The mind
may be the most amazing thing in the universe. In fact, as some scientists and
philosophers suggest, the mind IS the universe attempting to understand
itself. With all of this research and so much more we are learning much about
the brain and mind and also about the crucial and direct role that the brain
plays in happiness. And we have only begun to scratch the surface. Ramachandran speaks of the mysteries we face in contemplating it all:[18]

How can a three-pound mass of jelly that you can hold in your palm imagine
angels, contemplate the meaning of infinity, and even question its own place in
the cosmos? Especially awe inspiring is the fact that any single brain, including yours, is made up of atoms that were forged in the hearts of countless, far-
flung stars billions of years ago. These particles drifted for eons and light-
years until gravity and change brought them together here, now. These atoms
now form a conglomerate—your brain—that cannot only ponder the very stars
that gave it birth but can also think about its own ability to think and wonder
about its own ability to wonder. With the arrival of humans, it has been said,
the universe has suddenly become conscious of itself. This, truly, it the greatest mystery of all.

"Mystery" is a good word for it all and there are many things that remain
mysterious to us. Apart from their connections to our current inquiry on

happiness, these things are of intimate and inherent interest to us. The cosmos (the outer universe) continues to amaze but at the same time baffle us. Perhaps we should not be surprised since we have finite capacities and we are trying to understand the infinite. The mind (the inner universe), too, continues to elude our grasp. The precise connection between what we call the "brain" as opposed to the "mind" or "consciousness," for instance, has been debated from the time of Socrates and continues still.

A full summary of the various views is beyond our scope, the debate centers, however, around "materialist" and "non-materialist" views. Materialism traces to Ancient Greece with such thinkers as Democritus and Epicurus, and states that all things are ultimately made of matter. Today such theories as "physicalism," "mind-brain identity theory," and "reductionism" are the descendants of this view and hold that the mind is somehow reducible to the brain. Contemporary thinkers who hold this view include Daniel Dennet, W.V.N. Quine, Jerry Fodor, and many others. Non-materialist views are represented as well. "Dualism" (starting with Pythagoras and Plato) argues that the brain and mind are different sorts of things or substances, so that the mind cannot be reduced to the brain. The most famous proponent of dualism was 17th century French philosopher and mathematician Rene Descartes. Various versions of dualism are represented today in such thinkers as philosophers David Chalmers, Frank Jackson, John Polkinghorne, Jaegwon Kim, and many others. Other thinkers who reject materialism include Saul Kripke, Kurt Gödel (who has been called the greatest logician since Aristotle) and Thomas Nagel, who in his book *Mind and Cosmos: Why the Materialist Neo-Darwinian Conception of Nature Is Almost Certainly False,* argues that materialism fails in principle to explain features of mind such as consciousness and intentionality. [19]

There are many in the scientific community as well who reject materialism. Physicists Paul Davies and John Gribbon, for example, argue in their book *The Matter Myth* that materialism has in fact been disproven by quantum theory. [20] This is a view that was shared by the originator of this new physics, Max Planck, who argued: "There is no matter as such. All matter originates and exists only by virtue of a force that brings the particle of an atom to vibration and holds this most minute solar system of the atom together. We must assume behind this force the existence of a conscious and intelligent Mind. This Mind is the matrix of all matter." [21] Contemporary physicist Roger Penrose (an eminent physicist who, with his colleague Stephen Hawking, has advanced our understanding of black holes among many other mysteries of the cosmos) also argues in his book *The Emperor's New Mind* that the laws of physics fall short in attempting to explain capacities of the mind such as consciousness. [22]

These and many other mysteries seem locked inside the organ we are trying to understand—the human brain. Much more work is needed even to gain a sliver of knowledge in this area. Among the disciplines aiding in this quest is the science of psychology. Psychology has been of immense help, too, in our main inquiry here—the nature of happiness. In particular, a more recent focus called "positive psychology" has advanced our knowledge in this area and it is to this that we now turn.

NOTES

1. See Rick Hanson and Richard Mendius, *Buddha's Brain: The Practical Neuroscience of Happiness, Love and Wisdom* (Oakland, CA: New Harbinger Publications, 2009), 6. Also see Daniel J. Siegel, *Mindsight* (New York: Bantam Books, 2010), 38.

2. Daniel Kahneman, *Thinking: Fast and Slow* (New York: Farrar, Straus and Giroux, 2011), 21-22.

3. Ibid.

4. Plato, *Phaedrus,* in Hamilton, Edith and Cairns, Huntington trans., *The Collected Dialogues of Plato* (New Jersey: Princeton University Press, 1961), 246a-253e.

5. Paul Mclean, *The Triune Brain in Evolution* (New York: Plenum Press, 1990).

6. Stefan Klein, *The Science of Happiness: How Our Brains Make Us Happy—and What We Can Do to Get Happier* (New York: Marlowe and Company, 2006), 12-13.

7. Ibid.

8. Ibid.

9. Christopher deCharms: TED lecture "Inside the Brain," 2008, retrieved on 9/10/15: http://www.ted.com/talks/christopher_decharms_scans_the_brain_in_real_time.html

10. Jonathan Haidt, *The Happiness Hypothesis: Finding Modern truth in Ancient Wisdom,* (New York: Basic Books, 2006), 90-92.

11. Klein, *The Science of Happiness*, 37.

12. Jill Bolte. *My Stoke of Insight : A Brain Scientist's Personal Journey* (New York: Viking Press, 2009), 139.

13. Helen Fisher: TED lecture, "The Brain in Love" 2008. Retrieved on 9/10/15: http://www.ted.com/talks/lang/en/helen_fisher_studies_the_brain_in_love.html.Also see Helen Fisher: TED lecture "Why We Love and Cheat." 2006. Retrieved 9/10/15 http://www.ted.com/talks/helen_fisher_tells_us_why_we_love_cheat.html

14. V. S. Ramachandran: TED lecture "The Neurons that Shaped Civilization" 2009. Retrieved on 9/10/15: http://www.ted.com/talks/lang/en/vs_ramachandran_the_neurons_that_shaped_civilization.html

15. Douglas Hofstadter. *Gödel, Escher, Bach: An Eternal Golden Braid* (New York: Basic Books, 1979), 479.

16. Aristotle, *De Anima*, in Richard McKeon trans., *The Basic Works of Aristotle* (New York: Random House, 1941), Book 3.

17. C. G. Jung, *The Archetypes and the Collective Unconscious* (London, 1996).

18. V. S. Ramachandran, *The Tell-Tale Brain: A Neuroscientist's Quest for What Makes Us Human* (New York: W. W. Norton and Company, 2011).

19. Thomas Nagel, *Mind and Cosmos: Why the Materialist Neo-Darwinian Conception of Nature Is Almost Certainly False* (Oxford: Oxford University Press, 2012).

20. Paul Davies and John Gribbon, *The Matter Myth: Dramatic Discoveries that Challenge Our Understanding of Physical Reality* (New York: Simon and Schuster, 1992).

21. Max Planck. *"Das Wesen der Materie,"* (The Nature of Matter), speech given at Florence, Italy, 1944.

22. Roger Penrose, *The Emperor's New Mind: Concerning Computers, Minds, and the Laws of Physics* (Oxford: Oxford University Press, 1989).

Chapter Four

Happiness and Positive Psychology

Although "positive psychology" is said to have begun in 1998 with Martin Seligman's tenure as president of the American Psychological Association, it is not without historical influences.[1] There are some clear connections, at least in theoretical concepts, most notably to "humanistic" psychology. Abraham Maslow, after all, used the term "positive psychology" in his 1954 book *Motivation and Personality* and his emphasis on "self-actualization" clearly addresses areas of positive psychological health.[2] Some of Maslow's contemporaries made contributions as well. Erich Fromm,[3] for example, stresses the affirmative aspects of things like freedom and love on the personality, and Carl Rogers offered a "person-centered" approach, which attempts to help the client see his/her own uniqueness, individuality, and self-worth as an attempt towards gaining what he called "unconditional positive regard."[4]

So the connections between positive psychology and the humanistic tradition seem obvious enough. Brent Dean Robbins points out, for example, that Seligman has recognized Maslow and others as "distinguished ancestors" of positive psychology.[5] And Mihaly Csikszentmihalyi, another luminary in this field, has also acknowledged that some of the important concepts now being discussed were originally "assimilated within the humanistic tradition of Maslow and Rogers."[6]

What are some of the claims and findings of positive psychology? The claims for Seligman begin with his belief that the discipline of psychology has for too long operated from what he calls the "disease model."[7] It operates too often, that is, from the perspective of mental illness rather than mental health. He notes that there have been successes from the older perspective; namely as he states it "a science of mental illness has emerged," and there are now reliable treatments for more than a dozen mental disorders. But Seligman identifies the downsides of this one-sided approach. First, it leads to a

"victimology that ignores personal responsibility." Simply put, people become used to blaming this or that disorder for their own behaviors as if they
are determined to be the way they are. In so doing they attempt to avoid their
own freedom to change that behavior and do not hold themselves personally
responsible for it. Secondly, it takes our focus away from healthy, normal
lives, and from an examination of what really makes people happier. Positive
psychology focuses on strengths, not weaknesses. It attempts to find measurable qualities and traits that tend to lead to happiness. In tracking happier
people we find, for instance, that they are extremely social, prize friendships
and close personal relationships. Incidentally, it should be noted that Aristotle noted the importance of friendships as a key component of happiness long
ago.

Among the things positive psychology is learning is that certain character
strengths or virtues are tied to happiness and/or life satisfaction in important
ways. There is nothing totally new about this claim. Aristotle examined
character traits/virtues in the 4th ct. BCE. As we have seen he defined happiness in general as associated with good/virtuous character. But what is new is
that positive psychologists are attempting to provide the research and scientific rigor in this examination. For example Seligman and colleagues Nansook Park and Christopher Peterson have investigated a list of those character traits that seem most strongly and positively related to happiness, and
which ones seem less important. Zest for life, hope, gratitude, and love, for
example, seem to be among those rising to the top, whereas traits such as
modesty, intelligence and creativity seem to be lower among those things
that produce life satisfaction.[8] Incidentally, the idea that creativity is low on
the list may not be surprising given what we have learned about the brain. As
we have seen, the right hemisphere (which includes creative abilities) seems
to be a less happy region than the left.

Positive psychology has advanced our understanding of things like happiness and of some of its related components. One example is the important
concept of "flow," a term coined by Csikszentmihalyi.[9] Flow is described as
an intense, ecstatic state wherein one experiences complete involvement,
engagement or absorption with the activity at hand. In doing so a kind of
inner clarity and sense of deep purpose and fulfillment is achieved. Csikszentmihalyi sees this state as accessible to creative people as they pursue
solutions to a problem or obstacle in their work. He also notes a specific lack
of concern, under the state of "flow," for self, time, nutrition or physical
needs in general, because one is so dedicated and caught up in the work
itself. There are some key similarities, incidentally, between this notion of
"flow" and what Maslow called "peak experiences"[10] which are felt by self-
actualized people.

We also should not overlook the important contributions of social
psychologist Daniel Gilbert who addresses many important areas in his won-

derful book *Stumbling on Happiness*.[11] Gilbert engages us in what he calls "affective forecasting," which refers to the way in which we envision (usually wrongly, according to Gilbert) our emotional states in the future, namely, whether we will be happy under various circumstances. Most people would figure, he argues, that lottery winners will be happier than, say, paraplegics. But through time, according to Gilbert's research, both are equally happy. This is a surprising outcome to say the least. Gilbert's research shows us how true the cliché "time heals" really is. In addition we have what he calls a "psychological immune system"[12] which is largely unconscious and protects us from the severest kinds of negative, emotional damage. And the brain has a way of "synthesizing happiness" which, he says, is as real as real happiness. The brain does this by coming to terms with limitations on our freedoms and abilities, and finding a level of contentment within our situations in life. For these and other reasons, he argues, people are not very good at forecasting their own happiness.

When we remember Kahneman's research, which gives us reason to suspect and doubt our memories of past happiness, and combine it with Gilbert's "affective forecasting" results, it seems whether we are looking to the past or to the future we are simply not reliable recorders or predictors of our affective conditions.

Also, and surprisingly and contrary to the focus on freedom as a precondition for happiness we saw which developed in the Renaissance and Enlightenment periods, Gilbert's research shows that limitations on our choices do not seem to lessen our happiness, but in fact increase it. This has been shown in his experiments at Harvard University comparing students in one photography class who have more choices, and another with fewer choices. Those with fewer choices learned to become more content with the outcome of the class than those with more choices. Psychologist Barry Schwartz, too, provides analyses into this phenomenon in his book *The Paradox of Choice*.[13] Freedom of choice, he argues, can lead to unhappiness. Too many options can lead to paralysis and increased expectations and therefore make us less satisfied than if we had fewer options. This focus on the downside of freedom confirms the ideas from the existentialist philosophers (e.g., Kierkegaard, Nietzsche, Sartre) who argued that most people fear freedom, since with freedom comes responsibility for the choices made and most would rather ignore their own culpabilities.

More recently within the work of the founder of positive psychology Seligman himself, there has been a shift of focus. In his book, *Flourish*, Seligman has come to the recognition that it is not "happiness," in fact, that we should be examining (he refers to the old focus somewhat apologetically as "happyology"), but rather "flourishing" or "well-being."[14] In this he acknowledges an influence from Aristotle, namely, that the goal here needs to be *eudaimonia*, not *euphoria*. His current position is that too much attention has been paid to the simple view of happiness as a kind of pleasure, and that surely human life flourishes only when it includes things such as Aristotle discussed (namely virtues like courage and wisdom), in short, what we should be seeking is a meaningful life, rather than one simply guided by hedonic happiness.

With his shift in emphasis, Seligman deserves credit for acknowledging that there is something more than happiness in the usual sense that drives the human condition.[15] But what is this "something more than happiness"? It is to this question, finally, that we now turn.

NOTES

1. Martin Seligman's 1998 address as the President of the American Psychological Association can be read in full at: http://www.ppc.sas.upenn.edu/aparep98.htm

2. Abraham Maslow, *Motivation and Personality* (New York: Harper, 1954).

3. Erich Fromm, *The Art of Loving* (New York: Harper, 1956).

4. Carl Rogers, *On Becoming a Person: A Therapist's View of Psychotherapy* (London: Constable, 1961).

5. Brent Dean Robbins, "Positive Psychology and the Renaissance of Humanistic Psychology." *Humanistic Psychologist*, (2008), 36: 96–112.

6. J. Nakamura and Mihaly Csikszentmihalyi, *The Concept of Flow* (New York: Oxford University Press, 2005), 97.

7. Along with Seligman's APA 198 Presidential Address (referenced above) also see his TED talk "The New Era of Positive Psychology" (2004) found on 9/10/15: http://www.ted.com/talks/martin_seligman_on_the_state_of_psychology.

8. Martin Seligman, Nansook Park and Christopher Peterson, "Strengths of Character and Well-Being." *Journal of Social and Clinical Psychology*, Vol. 23, No. 5, (2004), 603–619.

9. Mihaly Csikszentmihalyi. *Flow: The Psychology of Optimal Experience* (New York: Harper, 1990).

10. Abraham Maslow, *Religions, Values, and Peak Experiences* (London: Penguin Books Limited, 1964).

11. Daniel Gilbert, *Stumbling on Happiness* (New York: Vintage Book, 2004).

12. Daniel Gilbert, TED Talk, "The Surprising Science of Happiness." (2005) Found on 9/10/15: http://www.ted.com/talks/dan_gilbert_asks_why_are_we_happy.

13. Barry Schwartz. *The Paradox of Choice: Why More is Less,* (New York: Harper Collins, 2004).

14. Martin Seligman, *Flourish: A Visionary New Understanding of Happiness and Well-being* (New York: Free Press, 2011).

15. A good source of current information on Seligman's ideas can be found at this website accessed on 9/10/15: http://www.authentichappiness.sas.upenn.edu/newsletter.aspx?id=54

II

The Wild Longing of the Human Heart:
The Search for Something More
Than Happiness

Chapter Five

Is Happiness the End We Seek?

We have now reached the point to directly confront the central question: whether happiness, after all, really is the *summum bonum* (the highest good) or, as Aristotle put it, whether happiness is the "end we all seek." In short is happiness the goal and purpose of human living? Before we can explore an answer to this question, however, we need to clarify two things.

Following Aristotle's lead we need to first clarify that we are not interested simply in *describing* what people *do* seek. Rather we desire to know whether we can *prescribe*, that is to say, whether we can we have some sense of what people *should* seek. It is the nature of philosophy to seek prescription rather than mere description, and we cannot deduce what should be the case, for instance, simply by examining how people do in fact behave. The daily news stories reveal, for example, many people behaving badly. People are capable of deceit, murder, and corruption of every sort. It is unfortunately easy to find many descriptions and examples of each. But we know that while people *do* in fact behave this way, that in fact they *should* not. We know, that is, that this behavior is not good. It is not good for them and it is not good for society. We know that they should not use deceit, they should not murder, and that people should avoid a life of corruption, and we know this not as a matter of description but of prescription. In other words our ideals are not based in simply observing human behavior. Our notions of what *ought* to be the case cannot be discerned simply from what *is* the case.

Second, we need to have an agreed upon understanding of what is currently meant by our key word "happiness." In our look at the brief history of happiness we saw that the term has meant different things to different people, cultures, and times. The working definition of happiness that I will employ here is what I take to be the most current and common, and what is sought after for the most part in the research examined in the last two chapters in positive psychology and brain science. Namely it is happiness considered as a psycho-physiological state and aligned with such feelings as contentment and tranquility. I consider this current view to have much in common with that proposed in the ancient world by Epicurus. In our brief survey we saw that the epicureans rejected the vulgar hedonism of Aristippus and others who sought after the base physical pleasures ("eat, drink and be merry, for tomorrow ye may die"), and replaced this with a more refined hedonism which focuses, rather, on the search for *ataraxia*, associated with feelings such as contentment, tranquility, peace of mind and the like. In short, this is happiness as *euphoria*.

It is true that we do desire this kind of happiness very much. We seem to reach for it like Tantalus, in the Greek myth, eternally reaches for food and drink. We seem to long for it. We seem to yearn after it. It is not surprising, then, that the most popular course at Harvard University has been one taught on the topic of happiness by professor Tal Ben-Shahar, author of the best-selling book *Happier*.[1]

Now that we understand these two things: our desire for prescription rather than mere description, and the modern sense of the word "happiness" that I am employing here, we can now address the central question whether happiness is, after all, the goal and purpose of human living. I think that when we begin to seriously examine this question we will find fairly quickly that despite its importance and attraction to us, happiness by itself alone cannot be the goal of human living or the highest good we should seek.

First and foremost and despite its draw for us, happiness cannot be the highest good simply because it is not intrinsically good at all. Let's agree to note, however, that for those who are chronically unhappy, such as those who suffer from depression, happiness is most definitely a good, but even in their case it is good as a means (an instrumental good which helps them get through the day, and not an intrinsic good) rather than as an "end in itself," to use Aristotle's terminology. The point is that happiness is not by itself a virtue. As a subjective psycho-physiological state, it is neither good nor bad. Happiness is neutral. Whether or not anything good or evil comes of it depends upon the events, circumstances and character of the persons involved, and happiness can be experienced by the just and the unjust alike. As Charles Gow once stated: "Many people are extremely happy, but are absolutely worthless to society."[2]

Consider the "Duchenne smile" we have discussed. We saw that this is a universally expressed outward sign of happiness. There are many examples of such a smile, however, on the face of evil people doing evil things. An example is the famous photo of a smiling Adolf Hitler after the capitulation of France, which was one more major victory on his way towards continued mass torture and murder. We can also see this same smile on the face of Mahatma Gandhi as he delighted in the end of the injustices of British colonialism in India, which was the cause he dedicated his life to. Indeed, it was the cause he lost his life for.

The Duchenne smile is revealed clearly on both faces. It reveals that both men are happy. So what does this tell us? The smile tells us something only of their internal states. But what is the relation each had to the outside world? Hitler's actions led to the mass murder of 12 million people and represent the very epitome of hatred and evil. His plan of *"die Endlösung"* (final solution) stood for the elimination of an entire race of innocent people he deemed "inferior." Gandhi's actions, on the other hand, are representative of a divine love and peaceful civil disobedience against injustice. His principle of *"sat-yagraha"* (the force of truth) stood for the elimination of injustice by means of non-violent resistance to evil, and went on to inspire others such as Martin Luther King Jr. in his struggle against the injustices of racial discrimination.

This comparison of Hitler and Gandhi is instructive. Let us get hold of the central issue and state it clearly. If a person has found the end of human living then that person can be said to have achieved something like Maslow's state of "self-actualization." That person can be considered a fulfilled human being. It follows that if happiness is the end we all should seek, then Hitler as well as Gandhi can be said to have reached that state of human fulfillment. But I think that every just and reasonable person understands that in a very important sense Hitler falls short of being a fulfilled human being. In fact, we could argue that in the moral sense Hitler falls short of being a human being at all. I think that a just and reasonable person understands that Gandhi serves as the better candidate for the self-actualized, fulfilled, human being, and that what makes him so has nothing to do with whether or not he was happy.

In understanding this we reach a key point and important understanding and it is this: *the end or goal of human living cannot simply be an internal, psycho-physiological state, such as happiness, and it therefore involves an individual's relationship to the external world.* Simply put, true human fulfillment is not achieved simply within *subjectivity* (an internal psycho-physiological state of the self), but rather is tied to *objectivity* (an external state measured by one's activities in the world outside the self). For Aristotle this external or objective pole is represented in the virtues themselves. This is why, as we have seen, he ultimately defined happiness as "activity of soul in accordance with virtue." Aristotle teaches us that the end we seek cannot be separated from virtue or goodness: as we have seen and it bears repeating: "Every art and every inquiry, and similarly every action and pursuit, is thought to aim at some good; and for this reason the good has rightly been declared to be that at which all things aim."[3] Living a fulfilled life, then, requires that we have a proper (virtuous) relationship to the external world.

Happiness by itself, and as a subjective state, need not have any real relation to the outside world at all. To understand this it will be instructive to consider the "Experience Machine" thought experiment introduced by philosopher Robert Nozick in his *Anarchy, State and Utopia.*[4] He asks us to imagine a machine that allows anyone plugged into it to experience the feeling of happiness. When connected to the machine we will feel the most sublime sense of accomplishment and tranquility, while in fact we are doing and accomplishing nothing real at all as we sit passively and alone in an empty room. We can imagine any virtual scenario and the machine will make it feel as if it is happening. One could order up the feeling of contributing something of importance to the world (of finding the solution to world hunger, say, or of disease). Or one could choose the experience of a loving relationship with the most beautiful and desirable person in the world or of enjoying the most sublime food and drink, or of climbing Mount Everest or of stopping all wars around the world. While connected to this machine, happiness would be felt intensely in this subjective state even though nothing at all is happening in the real world.

Nozick then raises the question whether or not we would choose to be connected to this machine. He thinks we would not, at least not for long periods of time and certainly not for the rest of our lives. He believes that regardless of potential disappointments we do seek after something real, even if it is not accompanied by happiness. In other words for Nozick, when it comes down to a battle between happiness and reality, reality wins. He believes that we want contact with the real world and with each other, even with all of the heartaches and failures that are possible. Remember, while connected to the machine we would forego any real accomplishments since nothing happens in reality and no outside purpose will be achieved. Of course we may be spared the possible failures that may come in trying to accomplish something in the real world. Perhaps the avoidance of this possible failure is part of the draw to the machine. But still and in short the question is whether we would sacrifice reality for an illusion. Nozick thinks not.

But what about you, do you agree? Would you want to be connected to the machine? Think about this carefully before you answer. This is a key question and your answer may reveal much about yourself and your own values. In our modern world there are many temptations that make such a machine appealing and attractive to us. We live in a world that seems to increasingly trade in reality for technology. Since the advent of the Internet, for example, we can choose to become "watchers" of life rather than "doers." We are granted access to almost any event anywhere in the world and nearly in real time. In many respects technology invites us to become simply *voyeurs* of life. We also live in a world of "virtual reality" and also "reality television," which is of course a contradiction in terms. In many respects, as noted by the French philosopher Gabriel Marcel, we are tempted by these and other technologies to become "spectators" rather than "participants" in life.

Before you decide whether you would agree to be connected to Nozick's Happiness Machine, let us also tinker with his thought experiment a bit since it may reveal a deeper issue. Suppose, for instance, that the machine has a mind of its own and delivers whatever experiences it chooses without respect to our own likes and dislikes. Let us further suppose that the machine has the ability to deliver the subjective state of happiness and tranquility regardless not only of the scenario, but also regardless of our true feelings in the real world. Some scenarios chosen by the machine may match your personal and moral preferences while others may not. Imagine further that the machine chooses the scenarios and not you. Suppose that it chooses inherently evil scenarios. For example, imagine a scenario whereby you virtually experience an innocent child being hurt or tortured and killed by a predator, but the feeling of happiness is delivered nonetheless. Again, in this thought experiment you would not be in control of what the actual experiences are, and while plugged into the machine you would feel happiness regardless and automatically.

Would you still want to be plugged into the machine? After all, no real child is being harmed. No real harm done, right? I would argue that a just and reasonable person would be rather uneasy about this situation and would reject the machine entirely. I think that such a person would know that the scenario is wrong and evil, even though nothing happens in reality, and that the mere thought of feeling happiness over such an evil act, even a virtual one, would be enough to bring disgust. I think this is enough to show that the subjective experience of happiness is not enough for us. There must be some connection to the outside world, to reality itself, to some objectivity, and to what Aristotle calls virtue.

We can also learn important things about why happiness fails to be the true goal of human living, when we consider lessons taught in Aldous Huxley's brilliant dystopian novel *Brave New World*.[5] In this work of fiction a horrifying picture of the future is presented. In this world a dictatorial regime controls our behavior with propaganda and technologies, while at the same time our individual happiness is delivered immediately and easily via a psychoactive drug called "soma." The moment the least bit of discomfort enters into our heads in this world, all we need do is pop a little soma, recite a few "hypnopaedic messages" (such as "a gram is better than a damn" – i.e., it is better to pop the fill and feel tranquility, than to put up with life's problems) and enjoy the ride into happiness, while the real affairs of the world around us are managed by "Controllers." In this brave new world the engines of society and mass production are ensured by encouraging consumers to discard old things, clothes, machines, etc., and to buy new ones—a thinking which is supported by hypnopaedic messages such as "ending is better than mending." Along with this kind of thought control, genetic engineering is used to provide stability for the community (we can engineer people content to pick up the garbage, and others to be our scientists, still others to be our soldiers and protectors, etc.). Would you want to live in such a world? After all, happiness would be assured, soma will do its work. Any moments of unhappiness would be easily replaced with tranquility and comfort.

Just as Nozick warns of the Happiness Machine, Huxley protested against the brave new world. In the end Huxley believed that we would lose freedom, truth, beauty, goodness, love and courage. In short, all that we prize as human beings would be sacrificed and destroyed in the name of soma-induced happiness. In a key exchange, Mustapha Mond (one of the powerful Controllers) is debating the novel's hero, John Savage, who is very much at odds with the brave new world's attempt to provide us comfort at the expense of our humanness. "We prefer to do things comfortably," argues Mond. Savage responds: "But I don't want comfort. I want God, I want poetry, I want real danger, I want freedom, I want goodness, I want sin." Mond responds with "In fact you're claiming the right to be unhappy," and Savage's reply provides the key line in the book: "All right then, I'm claiming the right to be unhappy."[6]

We should note that much of what Huxley warns us against is now actually happening. Neuroscience is zeroing in on psychoactive drugs to ward off all forms of unhappiness, so "soma" may not be far away. We are also well into the brave new world of genetic engineering. Also, techniques in the mass media and particularly through advertising are delivering messages in hypnopedic fashion and learning to take advantage of subliminal techniques as well. And many would argue that our governments are already watching over us and controlling our behavior. From Huxley's perspective we should reject the coming brave new world and choose real life instead, even with all of its potential problems, because only in real life will we have a chance to remain fully human.

Nozick and Huxley agree: happiness cannot be the end we all seek. We humans need something more. As we noted in the previous chapter, this fact has also been recently recognized by the father of positive psychology, Martin Seligman, who moves beyond his prior focus on happiness, which he now recognizes as overly simplistic, to address the higher ideal of human flourishing or well-being. "The time has finally arrived," he argues "for a science that seeks to understand positive emotion, build strength and virtue, and provide guideposts for finding what Aristotle called the 'good life.' "[7]

Again, after decades of looking at what he now calls "happyology," Seligman came to see what Aristotle saw more than 2,300 years ago, namely, what is more important than human happiness is human "flourishing" or "well-being,"—what he called *eudaimonia*. It is important to note that when Aristotle is so often quoted as saying that "happiness" is the "end we all seek," the actual word he uses and which has been translated as "happiness," is *eudaimonia*, which, as we have seen, is a Greek word that speaks to something far more than what we typically mean by "happiness." It speaks to flourishing, to fulfillment and to well-being, rather than to "happiness" as a mere psycho-physiological state of mind. And Seligman recognizes, as did Aristotle, that we need to move beyond this state when he writes "Well-being cannot exist just in your own head."[8]

So let us turn our attention, now, to a further examination of these things. What is needed for this "flourishing," "fulfillment," or "well-being"? What are its elements and its constituents, and how can it be achieved?

NOTES

1. Tal Ben-Shahar, *Happier: Learn the Secrets to Daily Joy and lasting Fulfillment* (New York: McGraw Hill, 2007).

2. Charles Gow's quote was retrieved on 9/10/15 from http://www.quotegarden.com/happiness.html.

3. Aristotle, *Nicomachean Ethics*, in Richard McKeon, trans., *The Basic Works of Aristotle* (New York: Random House, 1941), 1.1.

4. Robert Nozick, *Anarchy, State and Utopia* (New York: Basic Books, 1974).

5. Aldous Huxley, *Brave New World* (United Kingdom: Chatto and Windus,1932).

6. Ibid., Chapter 17.

7. Martin Seligman, *Authentic Happiness: Using the New Positive Psychology to Realize Your Potential for Lasting Fulfillment* (New York: Free Press, 2002), xi.

8. Martin Seligman, Flourish: A New Understanding of Happiness and Well-Being—and How to Achieve Them, (London: Nicholas Brealey, 2011), 14. More on Seligman's ideas are presented in the following websites accessed on 9/10/15: http://www.pbs.org/thisemotionallife/topic/happiness/what-happiness http://www.authentichappiness.sas.upenn.edu/newsletter.aspx?id=54

Chapter Six

Socrates and the Examined Life

John Stuart Mill once wrote: "It is better to be a human being dissatisfied than a pig satisfied; better to be Socrates dissatisfied than a fool satisfied."[1] This is ironic in light of the fact that, as we saw in chapter one, he is one of the fathers of a theory about happiness known as utilitarianism which claims that happiness is both a kind of pleasure and the end we all seek. Yet Mill recognizes the superiority of even an unhappy human life over that of a happy pig's life, and that even an unhappy Socrates is still better off than a happy fool. If an unhappy Socrates is better off it must be because there is something more than happiness that he pursued and that we all should be pursuing as well. It will serve us well, then, to briefly examine Socrates and what he pursued.

From all accounts Socrates was physically unattractive resembling a sa-tyr, with a short, fat, stubby build and a face with wide-set bulging eyes and an upturned nose with large nostrils. The force of his personality and his method in searching for wisdom, however, attracted many. Socrates did not claim to be wise and wrote nothing by his own hand because he believed that truth is found in dialogue rather than monologue. As for his own training in philosophy he gave credit to certain female philosophers and priestesses such as Aspasia and Diotima, with whom he was acquainted. He seems to have had a higher opinion of women than most of his contemporaries, and perhaps this had an influence on Plato, his most famous student, who would later call for equal education and opportunities for women in Greece; an extremely radical idea for its time. Socrates did his philosophizing in public places such as the market place, engaging any and all who would be willing to pursue it, always with an end to the "improvement of their souls" which, according to the famous legend, was the assignment given to him by the Oracle at Delphi (the priestess of Apollo).

Like his father, Socrates was a stonemason by trade and a good and noble citizen of Athens. When called upon he was also a brave soldier who defended Athens in times of war. Socrates fought during the Peloponnesian War (a nearly 30 year conflict between Greek city-states, wherein Sparta was ultimately victorious over Athens), as well as in many other battles. His bravery and valor are recounted in a number of Plato's dialogues. He also was selected as the Epistates (overseer or judge) of a trial involving famous Athenian generals charged with abandoning their troops during the Battle of Arginusae in 406 BCE. This may reveal the respect and trustworthiness his reputation had earned him. However since the government was now under Spartan rule, some Athenian loyalists may have seen Socrates as a kind of traitor. In any event the outcome of this trial was considered a miscarriage of justice and caused some to hold Socrates responsible calling for his arrest and execution. He did not succumb and escaped these threats, though the generals were eventually executed.

Still Socrates had much support. Many citizens considered him to be "the wisest man in Athens," in particular his younger contemporaries who were the aristocratic men destined to make up the coming generation of new Athenian leaders. From a historical perspective he was pivotal in the development of philosophy, which began in Greece around 600 BCE. Philosophers before Socrates (the Presocratics[2]) concentrated their efforts around understanding what the Greeks called *physis* (the physical world of nature). The first philosophers, then, were also the first scientists investigating the origins and nature of the *cosmos* (universe), and used *logos* (logic and reason) as their main tool (as we have seen, this is the origin of our present word "cosmology" referring to the study of the universe). These thinkers arrived at ideas quite startling for their time and are even consistent with some presently believed by modern scientists. Anaximander, for instance, argued that the universe is infinite with many worlds (an amazing idea for the time when most believed the universe was simply our Sun and the known planets) and gave us the earliest hint at a theory some see as consistent with evolution, arguing that the human race was somehow generated out of fish-like creatures. Heraclitus argued for a beginning of the universe that involved a huge "conflagration" (explosion or fire) that many have likened to the modern Big Bang theory. And similar to many scientists today who tell us that mathematics is the language of the universe, Pythagoras argued that the key to understanding the universe is through its mathematical structure. Finally, Democritus centered his attention on the make-up of the universe, claiming it is reducible to indivisible units of matter he called "*atoma*"—this is the origin of the atomic theory.

Socrates, however, shifted the focus of philosophy from a concern about the physical world (*physis*) to one centered on the study of the human person, in particular on the nature of the soul (*psyche*) itself. For this reason some contend that Socrates is rightly called the father of psychology (the study of *psyche*); in any case, he is credited with this very important shift in philosophy's concentration. Simply put Socrates brought one branch of philosophy to the forefront, namely ethics understood as the investigation into the *psyche*/soul and the examination of the just and good life, in short, how we should live our lives.

In his investigations Socrates relentlessly pursued a method of conversation and dialog (today known famously as the "Socratic Method") concerning the meaning and essence of enduring realities (truth, beauty and goodness) that he believed existed beyond the constant flux of the changing physical world. The Socratic Method is seen by some historians as the beginning of the scientific method in that it breaks down a subject into a series of questions generating hypotheses that are then tested by logic and reason. Karl Popper, one of the preeminent philosophers of science in the 20th century, saw Socrates' method as a kind of "intellectual intuition into the very eternal forms of truth, beauty and goodness themselves" leading to the "unveiling of the Great Mystery behind the common man's everyday world of appearances."[3] Socrates did often refer to intuition which he described as an inner voice or intuitive sense which he used as his *daemon* (guiding inner spirit or voice). Socrates' quest for knowledge was an inward journey. He believed that knowledge was possible and begins with his famous dictum: "know thyself." He also believed that knowledge can and does reveal truth. But what is truth, and how can we know it?

A key insight can be found in the nickname he gave to himself: "Socrates, the midwife of ideas."[4] His mother Phaenarete had in fact been an actual midwife helping to give birth to babies, and with this analogy Socrates reveals his belief that knowledge already lies inside each and every one of us (though in inchoate or undeveloped form), and that the question-answer style of the Socratic Method can help us to draw out/give birth to ideas that can clarify our understanding. Plato was to later use this as the foundation for his theory of innate ideas (the theory that some knowledge of truth, beauty and goodness already lies within our minds at birth). It is also interesting to note that the Socratic/Platonic view is reflected in the Latin source for the very word "education" itself, which is "*educare*" or "educe," i.e., "to draw out from what is already latently there in the mind."

In his quest for truth Socrates consulted with the greatest and most famous thinkers throughout all of ancient Greece. Plato provides a record of these conversations in his great works called the "Dialogues." In the end Socrates was never quite satisfied with any of the answers provided by many self-proclaimed experts called "Sophists" (wandering teachers claiming to be wise, who sold their "wisdom" for a price), and he was never shy in telling them so in eloquent though sometimes equally belittling fashion. He was also not afraid to point out inconsistencies and injustices committed by people regardless how famous and powerful they were.

Socrates was not afraid of making enemies and this along with a number of unfortunate events and misunderstandings led to his being brought to court on trumped-up and false charges of "impiety and the corruption of the youth." These were obvious lies and Socrates defended himself robustly and adequately as Plato's records in his *Apology* (the Greek *apologia* means "defense"). But Socrates had made too many enemies in high places and the misunderstandings were too ingrained. Contributing to this was "The Clouds," a well-known play about Socrates written by the famed playwright Aristophanes. Though a work of sarcasm and comedy, this play seems to have been taken by some as a more or less accurate portrayal of Socrates. It depicts him as a Sophist, and a thorn in the side of Athenian government and a critic of the traditional gods of Greece as well as a dangerous man who had poisoned the minds of the youth of Athens with philosophical nonsense. As he makes clear during his trial, Socrates believed the minds of many were biased against him because of this play and it would go on to contribute to the dire consequences for him.

In the end Socrates lost his battle in court. Under penalty of execution the judges required him to stop his trouble-making philosophizing. He was given the opportunity to avoid death if he would simply give up his philosophical quest and live a quiet and happy life (at 70 he was already an old man). Socrates responded with these now famous words: "the unexamined life is not worth living."[5] Tragically he was condemned to die by drinking poison from the hemlock plant in 399 BCE. His last conversations are recorded for us in Plato's *Crito*, and in it we see that Socrates died courageously and contently while pursuing wisdom until his very last breath. In Plato's *Phaedo* Socrates encourages his followers to pay less attention to his unfair demise and to pursue truth itself: "If you take my advice, you will give but little thought to Socrates but much more to the truth. If you think that what I say is true, agree with me; if not oppose it with every argument."[6]

The unfortunate end suffered by Socrates disturbed many throughout ancient Greece. His life and teachings had tremendous impact on Plato who gave up a promising political career and opened the first university in Western civilization called the Academy (it is where we get our word "academics"), in order to devote himself to philosophy and continue the Socratic search for those eternal realities: Truth, Beauty and Goodness.

Socrates can serve as the model for us all. He knew that there is something far more important than happiness. He could easily have escaped death by ending his quest. In fact it appears that some Athenian politicians and officials were fearful of negative consequences should the execution be carried out, so they bribed his prison guards and provided safe sanctuary to Socrates should he agree to escape. But he refused to go along with the plan.

He couldn't put an end to his philosophizing because this, in his mind, would be tantamount to intellectual or spiritual suicide. He believed he was on a divine mission to be the "gadfly" of Athens, and that it was his duty to carry it through. His was not a path towards earthly happiness. He did not wish just to live for living's sake, rather, he wanted to live a meaningful life and this required the search to continue.

But what constitutes a meaningful life? According to Aristotle,[7] Socrates was the first to search for universal truths and virtues. This search guides the content of Plato's *Dialogues* about Socrates' mission. In the *Meno* the search is for the nature of *virtue*; in the *Symposium* it is the nature of *beauty* that is desired; in the *Republic* it is the essence of *justice* itself which is sought after. However, are there really universal truths corresponding to these things and can we really come to know them? One well-known objection came from Protagoras, the most famous of all Sophists who laid claim to being "the wisest man alive." He wrote a text on "*Truth*" wherein he argues that each "man is the measure of all things: of the things that are, that they are, of the things that are not, that they are not." With these words Protagoras is considered the father of relativism, i.e., the view that there is no truth in the absolute sense, since truth is relative to the person and his/her perceptions.

Socrates believed that the Sophists were pretentious and dangerous charlatans who could make people believe almost anything as they sold their "wisdom" like food at the marketplace. We're told in Plato's *Protagoras* and *Theatetus* that Socrates attacked Protagoras' philosophy of relativism head on.[8] Since the claim is that knowledge is simply perception, he asks, why prefer human perceptions over that of an animal? Since animals perceive the world, perhaps a baboon's perception and therefore a baboon's truth is of equal worth to any human's? This may be seen as a silly retort. More serious problems emerge for relativism, however, since it seems to be self-refuting. In other words if no truth is absolute then relativism cannot be absolutely true either. Also, if truth amounts to nothing more than perception it follows that relativism will be both true and false at the same time, since some will perceive it to be true and others false. As Plato's greatest student Aristotle was to later argue in his *Metaphysics*, relativism violates a basic principle of logic (non-contradiction), since it would mean that statements could be both true and false at the same time.

Finally, if relativism were true would it not follow that everyone's perception (and therefore truth) would be of equal worth? If truth is merely perception, then no one person's truth could be more valuable than any other; no one could claim, then, to be wiser than another. This is a serious problem for any Sophist (who by definition accepts payment for his superior "wisdom") namely: why pay Protagoras for his wisdom? In demanding payment for their "wisdom" surely Protagoras and the other Sophists are implicitly claiming that their ideas are more valuable and better than others. Relativism therefore cannot be consistently maintained.

Many modern critics of relativism level a similar charge. Cognitive scientist and philosopher Noam Chomsky, for instance, argues that relativism cannot exist anywhere in ordinary life because it is "simply an incoherent theory."[9] Other important contemporary philosophers have also pointed out the self-contradictory and self-defeating nature of relativism, along with other problems, including Hillary Putnam, W.V. Quine and Martha Nussbaum. Quine states the argument this way: "Truth, says the cultural relativist, is culture-bound. But if it were, then he, within his own culture, ought to see his own culture-bound truth as absolute. He cannot proclaim cultural relativism without rising above it, and he cannot rise above it without giving it up."[10] Quine and Putnam famously defend a non-relativistic sense of truth (e.g., the reality of mathematical entities) in their "Quine-Putnam Indispensability Thesis." And Nussbaum defends an Aristotelian understanding of truth and goodness that she believes can be used to validly critique and evaluate societies as better or worse, contrary to the claims of relativism.

Despite such condemnations relativism is alive and well today. In fact, as American philosopher Allan Bloom argued, in contemporary society relativism is assumed as a kind of self-evident truth required of anyone who aspires to an open mind (for Bloom, however, relativism leads to the "closing of the American mind").[11] Besides this, relativism gets support from two major areas. First, it is supported within certain postmodern philosophers such as the French Continental thinkers Jacques Derrida, Michel Foucault, and Jean-Francois Lyotard, as well as the American philosopher Richard Rorty. Secondly, it is backed by modern "cultural relativism" which is a popular view among many anthropologists and social scientists in general. Let us look at each in their turn.

Postmodernism is the legacy of the father of atheistic existentialism Friedrich Nietzsche, who famously argued in his *The Will to Power* that "there is no truth" in the absolute sense because "truths are illusions" based on one's "perspective." Most famously, Nietzsche argues that "Truth" is:[12]

> A mobile army of metaphors, metonyms, and anthropomorphisms—in short, a sum of human relations which have been enhanced, transposed, and embellished poetically and rhetorically, and which after long use seem firm, canonical, and obligatory to a people: truths are illusions about which one has forgotten that this is what they are; metaphors which are worn out and without sensuous power; coins which have lost their pictures and now matter only as metal, no longer as coins.

Echoing Nietzsche's sentiment, Foucault claims that we have been lulled into believing in some absolute sense of truth because "truth is undoubtedly the sort of error that cannot be refuted because it was hardened into an unalterable form in the long baking process of history."[13] Foucault uses the term "episteme" (Greek for knowledge) to stand for his view that all of our knowledge claims are inevitably grounded in systems of our specific language, culture, and power and can only be perceived as true relative to those systems. Derrida's most popular phrase "there is nothing outside the text"[14] similarly suggests that our ideas are limited by language usage, which is irretrievably bound up with our culture and time. And Lyotard argues that the search for "the truth" is tied to "our nostalgia for the whole and the one"[15] which is a vestige of the past that we must now abandon. Rorty, on the other hand, arrives at his self-proclaimed postmodernism and relativism from a different route than the French Continental thinkers. He was first a well-known American analytic philosopher turned pragmatist, then towards the end of his career he became interested in postmodernism. Rorty embraces relativism and argues that we have "no organ for Truth, no Reason in the Platonic sense." Herein lies the common argument among postmodern/relativistic thinkers who deny there is any truth with a capital "T" (i.e., "Truth" in the absolute or non-relative sense), and who see Platonism as the enemy (since it carries on the Socratic search for such Truths). This contrariness dates back to Nietzsche who had a similar contempt for Platonism. Rather than search for Platonic Truths, Rorty argues we must be content with truths of the small "t" type, which can be defended by a "relativism, which relies on the common sense of the community to which one belongs."[16]

Can postmodernism survive Socratic criticisms any more than the Protagorean version of relativism? One central problem critics of postmodernism have noticed is very similar to the charge of inconsistency that Socrates levels at Protagoras. Lester Faigley is a scholar of postmodernism who notes that "the key assumption of postmodernism is that there is nothing outside contingent discourses to which a discourse of values can be grounded—no eternal truths, no universal human experience, no universal human rights."[17] But postmodern thinkers often adopt a normative stance, i.e., they reject some things as wrong and immoral. Derrida and Foucault, for example, consistently argue against the injustices of things like slavery, sexism, chauvinism, and the mistreatment of minority groups such as homosexuals. In doing so, surely, they are maintaining that such things are wrong in and of themselves—namely, that they are *intrinsically* wrong or evil. But if postmodernism is correct, it seems that all that we are justified in saying is that these things are wrong within the limits and boundaries of our current culture, and that we could, at least in principle, imagine different epochs, different cultures, different *epistemes,* wherein these things could arguably be defended. This seems to be an inherent inconsistency within postmodernism. Similar concerns have led Jürgen Habermas, a leading contemporary German philosopher and critic of relativism, to question the consistency of such normative claims made by Foucault and other postmodern thinkers. In fact,

Habermas refers to Foucault's normative claims as "cryptonormative,"[18] implying that they are often buried, concealed or otherwise go unnoticed within the prolific rhetoric of his postmodernism. In addition, Habermas argues that the relativism inherent in postmodernists like Foucault and Derrida makes the very act of communication problematic, since a commitment to truth seems to be a necessary requirement for communication in the first place.

Cultural relativism shifts the focus away from the Protagorean individual form of relativism (where each person him or herself is the measure of truth—today this is known as "subjectivism") to one that has its roots in culture itself. In the 5th century BCE Herodotus, the father of history, noted that behavior differs from one culture to the next (considering burial practices as an example) and proclaimed "Culture is king."[19] Following this tradition anthropologists in modern times, such as Franz Boas, have argued that "civilization is not something absolute, but relative, and our ideas and conceptions are true only so far as our civilization goes."[20] Since then many in his field have argued that cultural relativism is self-evident and that cultural differences are to be understood and tolerated from the perspective that each culture has its own customs and practices based on their uniquely held laws and morality, and that neither culture can be considered better or worse than the other, since "better" or "worse" can only be understood from inside the culture. Ruth Benedict and W. G. Sumner clarified this in their notion of "ethnocentrism" which stands for, according to Sumner, the mistake of judging another culture by virtue of the laws and morality of one's own culture. Margaret Mead did most to popularize the idea of tolerance towards cultures different from our own with her landmark book *Coming of Age in Samoa*, which is described in the preface as showing that "what constitutes courtesy, modesty, very good manners, and definite ethical standards is not universal. It is instructive to know that standards differ in the most unexpected ways."[21]

Can cultural relativism escape the Socratic critique? Many of the criticisms leveled at postmodernism would clearly still apply, but there are other problems as well. Philosopher Louis Pojman points out that a different sort of inconsistency is buried within the logic of cultural relativism. Namely, cultural relativists regard "intercultural tolerance" as a kind of self-evident prescription and duty. But as Pojman points out, this "view contains a contradiction. If no moral principles are universally valid, how can tolerance be universally valid?"[22] He also points out that cultural relativism would seem to entail that civil disobedience would always be wrong, since it runs against the prevailing moral views of one's culture (which according to the relativist's position is the "right" view). But it seems obvious that we all look approvingly to the courageous reformers who helped cultures in various parts of the world to remove unjust systems such as slavery, ethnic cleansing, mistreatment of women and minorities, and similar injustices. The very fact that we regard these as "injustices" implies we are on Socrates' side of things in seeing that they are universally wrong and unfair. Finally, Pojman notes that cultural relativism only focuses on differences rather than similarities between cultures. This is a limited and biased view since it only gives us one side of things. Cultures do, in fact, agree on many things as well. For instance all cultures define "murder" as a form of unjustifiable killing; all cultures oppose things like incest and lying; all cultures promote living up to one's obligations, etc. We could also add that cultures, through their religious beliefs, universally recognize the "Golden Rule" which many see as the founding principle for all ethical behavior.

Consider the following examples provided in the major faiths and religions around the world:[23]

> Hinduism: This is the sum of duty; do naught onto others what you would not have them do unto you.
> Buddhism: Hurt not others in ways that you yourself would find hurtful.
> Taoism: Regard your neighbor's gain as your own gain, and your neighbor's loss as your own loss.
> Confucianism: Do not do unto others what you would not like yourself.
> Zoroastrianism: That nature alone is good which refrains from doing to another whatsoever is not good for itself.
> Judaism: What is hateful to you, do not do to your fellowman. This is the entire Law; all the rest is commentary.
> Christianity: All things whatsoever you wish that men do unto to you, do so unto them, for this is the law and the prophets.
> Islam: No one of you is a believer until he desires for his brother that which he desires for himself.

Postmodernism and cultural relativism pose challenges to the Socratic search for Truth, Beauty and Goodness, but they both face similar challenges to those Protagoras faced when confronted by Socrates. The mission of Socrates lives on. His legacy is continued through Plato's philosophy, an important linchpin of Western civilization. As the eminent mathematician and philosopher Alfred North Whitehead once remarked: "the safest general characterization of the European philosophical tradition is that it consists of a series of footnotes to Plato."[24]

But the Socratic influence has gone far beyond philosophy.[25] The British Romantic poets, for instance, saw Socrates as the ideal model for intelligent and moral behavior. Shelly calls him "the Jesus of Greece," and in his letters Keats compares him with Jesus as well. Many of the framers of America, too, highlighted his importance. Madison and Jefferson spoke of him in the highest terms, and Benjamin Franklin suggests that the surest way to the practice the virtue of humility is to "imitate Jesus and Socrates." The connection to Jesus is no doubt a tribute to the fact that he, too, was willing to die for what he believed in. In doing so, Socrates became the Martyr of Philosophy.

Socrates is also seen as the father of civil disobedience. His ideas directly influenced the thought and actions of such courageous people as Thoreau who, like Socrates, accepted unjust penalty as a way of highlighting injustice; Gandhi, who translated Plato's *Apology* into his native language and called Socrates a "Soldier of Truth"; Mandela, who made use of "Socratic education" while imprisoned in South Africa; and finally Martin Luther King Jr., who in his "Letter from Birmingham Jail" writes: "To a degree, academic freedom is a reality today because Socrates practiced civil disobedience."

The Socratic search for Truth, Beauty and Goodness still drives us forwards and is as valid today as it was in ancient Athens. They form the key component of the "wild longing of the human heart." But what are these things? What are Truth, Beauty and Goodness? It is to this question that we must now turn.

NOTES

1. John Stuart Mill, *Utilitarianism* (London: Parker, Son and Bourn, 1863), Chapter Two.

2. For more on the Presocratics, see W.K.C. Guthrie, *A History of Greek Philosophy* (Cambridge: Cambridge University Press, 1962).

3. Karl Popper, *The Open Society and its Enemies* (London: Routledge & Kegan Paul, 1945), 133.

4. Plato, *Theatetus*, in Hamilton, Edith and Cairns, Huntington trans., *The Collected Dialogues of Plato* (New Jersey: Princeton University Press, 1961), 149-151.

5. Plato, *Apology*, in Hamilton and Huntington (1961), 37e-38a.

6. Plato, Phaedo, in Hamilton and Huntington (1961), 91b-c.

7. Aristotle, *Metaphysics*, in Richard McKeon trans., *The Basic Works of Aristotle* (New York: Random House, 1941), Book One.

8. Plato, *Theatetus*, in Hamilton and Huntington (1961), 152a.

9. Noam Chomsky's critique is last retrieved on 9/10/15 from the following website: https://www.youtube.com/watch?v=pt2fdivw4cs.

10. W.V.N. Quine, quoted in H. Siegel, *Relativism Refuted: A Critique of Contemporary Epistemological Relativism* (Dordrecht: D. Reidel, 1987), 43.

11. Allan Bloom, *The Closing of the American Mind* (New York: Simon and Shuster, 1987), Preface.

12. Friedrich Nietzsche, "On Truth and Lies in the Nonmoral Sense," in Walter Kaufmann, trans. *The Portable Nietzsche* (New York: Viking Press, 1960), 46-47.

13. Michel Foucault, "Nietzsche, Genealogy, History," D. Bouchard and S. Sherry, trans., in *Language, Counter-Memory, Practise*, ed. D. Bouchard (Ithaca, N.Y.: Cornell University Press, 1977), 143.

14. Jacques Derrida, *Of Grammatology*, Gayatri Chakravorty Spivak, trans., (Baltimore: Johns Hopkins University Press, 1976), 158.

15. Jean-Francois Lyotard, "What is Postmodernism?" in *Art and It's Significance*, Stephen David Ross, editor (New York: State University of New York Press, 1994), 561-565.

16. Richard Rorty, "Hermeneutics, General Studies and Teaching," printed in *Classic and Contemporary Readings in the Philosophy of Education* (New York: State University of New York Press, 1997), 522-536.

17. Lester Faigley, *Fragments of Rationality: Postmodernity and the Subject of Composition* (Pittsburgh: University of Pittsburgh Press, 1992).

18. Jürgen Habermas, *The Philosophical Discourse of Modernity: Twelve lectures* (Cambridge: MIT Press, 1987), 266-293.

19. Herodotus (c. 450 BCE), *History of the Persian Wars*, translated by David Grene (Chicago: University of Chicago Press, 1985).

20. Franz Boas, "Museums of Ethnology and their classifications." *Science* 9, (1987): 589.

21. Margaret Mead, *Coming of Age in Samoa* (New York: William Morrow Paperbacks, 1928).

22. Louis Pojman, *Introduction to Philosophy* (New York: Oxford University Press, 2004), 493.

23. "The Golden Rule:" retrieved on 9/10/15 at http://www.teachingvalues.com/golden-rule.html.

24. Alfred North Whitehead, *Process and Reality* (Free Press, 1979), 39.

25. Final quotes about Socrates for the rest of this chapter are found in Debra Nails, "Socrates," *The Stanford Encyclopedia of Philosophy, 2014,* retrieved on 9/10/15 from: http://plato.stanford.edu/entries/socrates/

Chapter Seven

The Search for Truth, Beauty, and Goodness

Albert Einstein once remarked: "the ideals which have always shone before me and filled me with the joy of living are goodness, beauty, and truth. To make a goal of comfort or happiness has never appealed to me; a system of ethics built on this basis would be sufficient only for a herd of cattle."[1] Like Socrates, Einstein understood that a fulfilling and meaningful human life looks beyond mere satisfaction or happiness and towards the pursuit of truth, beauty, and goodness. These are the key values for human living. They attract us towards them as if by magnetic force. But what are they, and can we hope to completely understand them?

We must have a primitive and intuitive understanding of them or else we would not seek after them in the first place. In this way truth, beauty and goodness may be like what Aristotle called "first principles"[2] which cannot and need not be fully explained, demonstrated, or defined. By example, in his works on logic he explains our attempt to gain knowledge through definitions:

> Our own doctrine is that not all knowledge is demonstrative: on the contrary, knowledge of the immediate premises is independent of demonstration. (The necessity of this is obvious; for since we must know the prior premises from which the demonstration is drawn, and since the regress must end in immediate truths, those truths must be indemonstrable). Such, then, is our doctrine, and in addition we maintain that besides scientific knowledge, there is its originative source which enables us to recognize the definitions.[3]

What Aristotle is discussing here is known today as the "epistemic regress problem" of knowledge. If we require, that is, all claims to be defined and demonstrated before we can accept them as true, this leads us down a path backwards from which there is no escape. By analogy we can argue that we will accept Z as true if and only if Z can be demonstrated by some other truth, Y. But then, of course, the same justification for Y would be required, which leads us to X, which relies upon the truth of W, and so on. We will have to carry this procedure out until we reach A. But what about A, how do we know it is true? If we require that A also be demonstrated we will need to supply new evidence Z1, which will lead us to Y1, then X1, and W1, all the way down to A1. But then A1 will be in need of demonstration, too, so we shall need to start over again with yet more evidence starting with Z2, eventually getting down to A2, and the same process will start all over again and continue backwards forever with no end.

This problem gives us limited options. Either we embrace skepticism and deny that knowledge is possible at all since we are caught in the infinite regress backwards, or we see the logic of Aristotle's way out in recognizing that there are certain "first principles" coming from some "originative source" that we can know as a basis and foundation for all other knowledge moving forwards. But how will we know that these "first principles" are true? Aristotle reasons that such truths are either self-evident or intuitively understood.

This may be disconcerting to some but there is good reason to believe that Aristotle is right. Kurt Gödel, the greatest logician since Aristotle, published his "Proofs of Incompleteness" in 1931, which showed that there are truths that can never be proven or demonstrated within any system. Gödel was speaking here about mathematical and logical truths, but perhaps we can see that something analogous occurs with any attempt to provide demonstrable knowledge of our key values: truth, beauty and goodness.

In fact G.E. Moore, one of the pioneers of analytic philosophy at the beginning of the 20th century, defends this very idea. He argues that things like goodness and beauty are "intrinsic values" that we understand but cannot completely define or demonstrate.[4] Since they are "intrinsic" they do not need nor admit of demonstration, for by definition their worth and value is not reliant on something outside them. As an example he argues that any attempt to define something like goodness commits "the naturalistic fallacy." Suppose, he argues, someone tries to define it in terms of some natural property such as "goodness is pleasure." For Moore such a claim leads to the "open question" argument, namely, it is reasonable to ask "is pleasure good?" This means that "goodness" must logically contain something distinct from "pleasure." Compare this, for example, with a definition of "bachelor" with something like "a bachelor is an unmarried male." This claim is not subject to the open question argument since the question "is an unmarried male a bachelor?" would be contradictory. Moore goes on to argue, then, that all such attempts to define goodness and beauty will fail due to the naturalistic fallacy, and that our knowledge of them is based on a form of intuition.[5]

Though our understanding of truth, beauty, and goodness may be intuitive and may never admit of full demonstration or definition, still we can learn a great deal about them from a variety of sources. These values, after all, have a long tradition in the history of philosophy beginning with the 6th century BCE philosopher Parmenides, who saw them as properties of being or reality itself.[6] Today this view is known as Platonism, since Plato was the first thinker to develop a theory proposing that they have independent existence outside of human minds. They are, he argued, eternal realities that lie in a realm that transcends the spatial-temporal world. For this reason they are often referred to as the "Transcendentals." For Plato they constitute the main "Forms" of being that are somehow embedded into the fabric of the universe itself.

As we saw in the last chapter Platonism was criticized by Nietzsche and the postmodern philosophers. Platonism has, however, been defended by many philosophers such as A.N. Whitehead, W.V.N. Quine, Hillary Putnam, Thomas Nagel, and Rebecca Goldstein. It has also found support among scientists such as the eminent physicist Werner Heisenberg (discoverer of the "Uncertainty Principle" within quantum physics) who once remarked:

"I think that modern physics has definitely decided in favor of Plato. In fact the smallest units of matter are not physical objects in the ordinary sense; they are forms, ideas which can be expressed unambiguously only in mathematical language."[7]

And more recently physicist Roger Penrose has defended the Platonic belief in the independent reality of universals such as mathematical truths, as well as beauty and morality in his books *The Emperor's New Mind* and *The Road to Reality*. Penrose states his view unequivocally:[8]

> Plato speaks of truth, beauty and morality, but in my view, truth in its purest form tends to be mathematical truth. However, I'm somewhat sympathetic towards a broader Platonism in which morality and beauty have fundamental elements which are also absolute and independent of individuals or cultures.

Likewise most mathematicians have a special regard for Platonism.[9] In part this is due to an appreciation of the important impact that mathematics had on Plato's overall philosophy (principally through the influence of the Pythagoreans). He believed that mathematics was the model for all knowledge, which accounts for the famous words engraved above the entrance to his great school, the Academy: "let no one ignorant of mathematics enter here." What Plato saw was that mathematical truths seem to offer us a kind of bridge between this physical world and the world of the Forms. Today this view is known as Mathematical Platonism and it is defended by, among others, Kurt Gödel, W.V.N. Quine, Hillary Putnman, and René Thom, who stated that "mathematical forms have an existence independent of the mind considering them,"[10] and Georg Cantor (the inventor of set theory) who also was a "Platonist, a believer that mathematical reality transcends the human mind."[11]

Though the majority of mathematicians agree with this view, the case made against Platonism is called "Formalism," which argues that mathematics is simply a formal system based on mathematical formulas that we have invented through time as useful ways to understand our world. A pioneer of this theory was the brilliant German mathematician David Hilbert in the late 19th and early 20th centuries. This view sees mathematics as simply a set of formulas and rules equivalent to an advanced and hyper-complex game of chess. Accordingly math does not reveal anything embedded in reality at all, but rather is an ingenious invention of the human mind. However, most philosophers of mathematics agree that Kurt Gödel's Proofs of Incompleteness dealt a fatal blow to formalism by showing that formal systems are incomplete since they cannot account for all mathematical truths. There are truths, in other words, that lie outside any formal systems that try to describe or prove them. How is it, then, that we can know them to be true? Gödel expresses his Platonic views as follows:[12]

> Despite their [mathematical truths] remoteness from sense experience, we do have something like a perception also [for example] of the objects of set theory, as seen from the fact that the axioms force themselves upon us as being true. I don't see any reason why we should have less confidence in this kind of perception, i.e., in mathematical intuition, than in sense perception . . . They, too, may represent an aspect of objective reality.

Many contend that Formalism also faces another more obvious problem. If mathematics is simply human construction of formulas, why is it so effective in revealing an understanding of the physical world? Physicist Eugene Wigner once referred to this problem as "the unreasonable effectiveness of mathematics in the natural sciences," [13] which demands some sort of explanation. In other words how and why does math describe nature so well? How does math lead to such astounding empirical predictions such as Einstein's $E = mc^2$, or, more recently, the discovery of the Higgs boson particle based on the mathematical predictions of Peter Higgs? And how and why does mathematics find so much order in the world? We now know that order is found to exist even in the most complex features of the physical world. This is due to the discoveries of Benoit Mandlebrot who used a new form of mathematics (fractal geometry) in order to better understand the mathematics of "roughness" (things which have no fine shapes or lines, such as clouds, islands, mountain ranges, etc.). What he discovered (and Mandlebrot specifically states they were discovered and not invented) was a great deal of order within seeming chaos, and simplicity within complexity, which has important applications to physics, biology, medicine and even the stock market.[14] Ancient Greek thinkers seem to have been correct after all, in naming the universe the *cosmos* (order). So what is the explanation for the overwhelming effectiveness of mathematics? Platonism's answer is that it is further evidence that mathematics is not simply human construction or invention but, rather, it leads to discoveries of truths embedded in reality itself.

While this debate continues on, mathematics also seems to lend its support for another idea within Platonism. Plato regarded truth, beauty and goodness as also somehow connected and related to each other. This is an interesting idea. Ralph Waldo Emerson stated it plainly: "Truth, and goodness, and beauty, are all but different faces of the same All."[15] The relationship between truth and beauty has a long-standing tradition among poets and artists who recognize their connection as a form of creative insight. British Romantic poet, John Keats, for example, famously writes in his "Ode on a Grecian Urn":[16] "Beauty is truth, truth beauty—that is all Ye know on earth, and all ye need to know." American Romantic poet Emily Dickinson also concurs with her own poetic expression:[17]

> "I died for Beauty—but was scarce/Adjusted in the Tomb/When One who died for Truth, was lain/In an adjoining Room./He questioned softly, 'Why I failed'?/'For Beauty,' I replied—/'And I—for Truth—themselves Are One—/ We Brethren, are,' He said."

The artistic understanding of the connection between truth and beauty found in Keats and Dickinson may be a form of intuition and as such is consistent with Plato's belief in the theory of innate truths—i.e., that the mind is not a blank slate or *tabula rasa*, but rather possesses knowledge from within, though in an inchoate and undeveloped state. According to this theory knowledge is "brought out from" the mind and developed, further understood, and communicated more fully as we live out our lives. As we noted in the previous chapter, our word "education" is Platonic in the sense that it is derived from the Latin "*educere*" (to "educe" or draw out from). Plato makes this case most directly in his *Meno*, with the story of an illiterate slave boy who is able to deduce fairly complex mathematical truths when asked the proper questions, even though he had no mathematical training.[18]

A modern example of this idea is provided within Mandlebrot himself, namely, when he first saw the visual representation of his famous set. It is known as the "Mandelbrot set" which incidentally, according to Penrose, supports Platonism: "I don't see any other way of really understanding what the Mandelbrot set is about," Penrose states, "other than that there is something out there, a Platonic notion, which we can explore through greater degrees with the greatest skills we have."[19] In Mandelbrot's case, upon first seeing the colored computer images of fractals generated by his famous M-set, he records feeling a strange familiarity with the many shapes. He reasoned that this is due to the fact that they appear in so much artistic work he has experienced from around the world. Mandelbrot suggests that artists must have an intuitive understanding of the fractals, even without understanding one thing about mathematics. [20]

There is an interesting comparison to be made here, too, with the eminent psychologist C. J. Jung's notion of the "archetypes," which exist, he argued, innately as patterns in the collective unconscious mind of us all. In particular Jung was most fascinated with *mandalas*—symbolic and artistic representations of the universe found within Hinduism and Buddhism as well as throughout many cultures—which bear a striking resemblance to the Mandelbrot set. [21]

Whatever this artistic/intuitive understanding is, we can look to mathematics for further confirmation of the connection between truth and beauty. Some have argued that mathematics has nothing to do with beauty, but as Aristotle points out in his Metaphysics "those who assert that the mathematical sciences say nothing of the beautiful or the good are in error . . . The chief forms of beauty are order and symmetry and definiteness, which the mathematical sciences demonstrate in a special degree." [22] In the Western world the relationship of beauty to mathematical proportion and symmetry goes back as far as the 6th century BCE, when Pythagoras gave us his famous theorem $(a^2 + b^2 = c^2)$ which he admired for its own inner beauty. He is also credited with the discovery that pleasing musical sounds (e.g., on stringed instruments) are related to mathematical ratios (e. g., unison=1:1; octave=2:1; perfect fifth=3:2). [23] Another example from the ancient world is the famous "golden ratio" (considered to be the most aesthetically pleasing mathematical proportion known, represented as a ratio of, roughly, 1.61). Physicist Mario Livio argues that this ratio was known as early as Euclid, [24] and that it was also used by architects in the ancient world to design such things as the pyramids and the Parthenon. Knowledge of the golden ratio was also used, Livio claims, by artists such as Leonardo DaVinci and Salvador Dali and fascinated scientists such as Johannes Kepler. It is also said to be embodied in nature itself in things such as pinecones, mollusk shells, rose petals, and even in the shape of our Milky Way galaxy. [25] Similar claims are made for the number "Pi" (a ratio of a circle's circumference to its diameter, represented as π and is approximated at, roughly, 3.14159), as well as in the Fibonacci numbers (named after the 13th century Italian mathematician, which are represented as a sequence arrived at by adding together the previous two numbers: 1, 1, 2, 3, 5, 8, 13, 21, 34, 55, 89, and so on). Both of these mathematical discoveries, known by ancient mathematicians as well, are also found represented in nature just like the golden ratio.

Among more modern mathematicians, too, the connection between truth and beauty finds much support. Famed mathematician/logician Bertrand Russell also noted "mathematics, rightly viewed, possesses not only truth, but supreme beauty."[26] The brilliant Hungarian mathematician Paul Erdős similarly wrote: "Why are numbers beautiful? It's like asking 'why is Beethoven's Ninth Symphony beautiful?' If you don't see why, someone can't tell you. I *know* numbers are beautiful. If they aren't beautiful, nothing is."[27] Nobel Prize winning mathematician Paul Dirac, too, refers to the "great mathematical beauty" of equations such as those used to support Einstein's theory of relativity. He was firmly convinced that the beauty of an equation is also good evidence of its truth (a point that Einstein himself often made) and once remarked "it is more important to have beauty in one's equations than to have them fit experiment." Some of Dirac's own equations came from "playing around with pretty mathematics" as he put it, and led to ideas that are now foundational in the field of physics.[28] S. Chandrasekhar, winner of the Nobel Prize for his theories on the evolution of stars, so noticed the relationship between truth and beauty that he dedicates and entire text to the subject entitled *Truth and Beauty: Aesthetics and Motivations in Science*.[29]

So the Platonic connection between truth and beauty has found much support within the arts, sciences, mathematics, and philosophy, but what can be said of the relationship between truth and goodness? At first, it seems, there are no connections. Logicians, for example, see truth simply as a property of statements. If the content of the statement corresponds with reality (e.g., "you are reading this sentence right now") then that statement is considered true—this is known as the "correspondence theory of truth." If a statement is coherent with other things known to be true (e.g., "people who read books tend to be more informed than those who do not") then it is also considered true—this is known as the "coherence theory of truth."[30]

Within logical truth there does not seem to be any apparent connection to goodness. But we may be helped here if we remember the mission of Socrates. Was he in search of logical truth? To some extent the answer is yes. Much of his quest directly involved investigating logical answers to his many provocative questions (e.g., "What is Justice?"). However, was this the sense of truth that Socrates died for? Certainly not, Socrates risked his life for a special kind of truth that ethicists call "moral truth." During most of his life he gave much effort to examining moral questions. As we saw in his confrontation with the relativism of Protagoras, Socrates argued that some things are clearly better and truer than others, and this includes moral truths such as "a just society is better than an unjust one." It is important to note that for Socrates (just as for Plato) moral truths have something in common with mathematical truths—namely, they are not merely mental constructs or inventions of the human mind, rather, they reveal truths embedded in the universe itself. As indicated earlier, this view finds support in thinkers such as physicist Roger Penrose. It also has been defended by philosopher Thomas Nagel in his *Mind and Cosmos*, which advocates a view of moral truth that has "pre-existed us as a kind of Platonic form, into which we are gradually growing, as we discover morality the way we discovered the Pythagorean theorem" and "that certain deeds would be wrong whether humans thought so or not, and this structure of morality must have existed independently before conscious minds started musing over it."[31]

We have also seen that this view of moral truth is criticized by cultural relativism. But relativism is self-refuting, contradictory, and unable to account for even the simplest of moral truths such as "a just society is better than an unjust one." In addition I believe that relativism is subject to Moore's "open question argument." Relativism argues that morality is simply whatever a society chooses it to be. But clearly we are still able to question whether the values selected by that society are in fact moral. For example suppose that in society X it is considered right, good, and moral to enslave women and children, murder innocents for pure sport, use deception rather than honesty, and practice discrimination against those considered different in matters such as sexual orientation or race. Clearly we can ask whether these values are good or evil, and this shows—using Moore's reasoning—that morality cannot be defined simply as whatever a society chooses. And if we choose to criticize the values chosen by society X, as we clearly should, relativism will be useless to us. There is no basis for criticism provided. The beliefs and practices of society X are simply the values chosen by that society, and the rest of us are simply required, according to relativism, to exhibit understanding and even tolerance.

However, I think we understand that any just person or society would clearly recognize another option, and that is that moral truths, like mathematical truths, are not chosen, created, or invented by societies at all. We would see that societies like society X have simply made serious moral mistakes. And rather than be tolerant of it all, I think we would feel morally obliged to help society X see the error of its ways and help defend the rights of the victims within it. Furthermore, if the injustices of society X began to extend beyond its borders and threaten to infect others and our own world, I think we would then address it in a more serious way, which is what civilized nations did in WW2, for example, against the evils and injustices of Nazism.

In thinking of Nazism as an example, we might also gain some insight into another of Plato's claims, namely that goodness is somehow "higher" than truth (Plato states that the highest of the Forms is the "Form of the Good.").[32] Consider, for example, the age-old moral question: is it ever morally right to tell a lie? If we imagine that we are hiding Anne Frank and her family in the attic of our home during the horrors of Nazi Germany, for example, we can wonder what we will feel morally bound to do if the Gestapo comes knocking at our door seeking out innocent Jews to be slaughtered.

If he asks whether we are aware of any Jews hiding in the city, shall we feel some blind loyalty to truth telling and answer, "yes, in fact a Jewish family is now hiding in our attic"? Or do we recognize an allegiance to a higher truth—namely, the moral truth that no one has the right to destroy innocent lives? It seems clearly and morally reasonable for a just person to lie to the Gestapo in such a case. I would also argue that it would be, in fact, our moral duty to do so. We could argue that from a moral perspective the Gestapo does not deserve to be told the truth because he is a member of a society which has chosen its values wrongly—i.e., it has chosen evil over goodness. In this way we can understand, I think, not only that relativism is wrong (since it is possible for a society to choose the wrong values) but also that Plato was correct in his claim that goodness is higher than truth, or, to put it another way, moral truth is a higher kind of truth.

Einstein, too, recognized that moral truths are more important than other kinds of truth when he wrote: "Humanity has every reason to place the proclaimers of high moral standards and values above the discoverers of objective truth. What humanity owes to personalities like Buddha, Moses, and Jesus ranks for me higher than all of the achievements of the enquiring and constructive minds."[33] Einstein understood that a blind allegiance to the search for truth in science could lead to great dangers. "Since the splitting of the atom," he once proclaimed, "everything has changed except our way of thinking. And thus mankind drifts toward catastrophe. If humanity is to survive it shall require a new way of thinking." He was convinced that this new way of thinking would require that our lives be led by moral truth: "the most important endeavor is the striving for morality in our actions. Our inner balance and even our very existence depend on it."[34]

The man Einstein most admired in his own time was Mahatma Gandhi, the greatest moral leader of his day. As we have seen Gandhi led the independence movement in India, which was suffering under oppressive British rule. Einstein was impressed with Gandhi's sense of moral truth which was called "*satyagraha*" (translated as "holding on to the truth" and "the force of truth"). It came to represent Gandhi's philosophy of peaceful, non-violent resistance to injustice, a philosophy inspired by Socrates and, in turn, one which inspired the civil disobedience movement of Martin Luther King, Jr. Of Gandhi Einstein once said "Generations to come, it may well be, will scarce believe that such a man as this one ever in flesh and blood walked upon this Earth," and when Gandhi was murdered by an assassin's bullet in 1948, Einstein continued: "I believe that Gandhi's views were the most enlightened of all political men of our time. We should strive to do things in his spirit: not to use violence in fighting for our cause, but by non-participation in anything you believe is evil."[35]

Gandhi was the Socrates of his time. He knew there were truths that made life worth living. He also embraced truths worth dying for. He once wrote that "the quest for Truth involves self-suffering, sometimes even unto death."[36] We see truth and goodness embodied in Gandhi's life and death. Inspired by Gandhi, Einstein once remarked that it is "only morality in our actions [that] can give beauty and dignity for life."[37]

But what does it mean to refer to Gandhi's life as "beautiful"? In examining this, perhaps we can hope to understand the final connection needed among our key values—that between beauty and goodness. Certainly we have, again, a kind of intuitive understanding of the truth of a statement like "Gandhi lived a beautiful life." I think also that we would immediately and intuitively reject a statement such as "Hitler lived a beautiful life" as utterly and completely false. It seems that the difference here lies in the fact that Gandhi's life was beautiful because it was guided by truth and goodness, and that Hitler's life was devoid of truth and goodness, and therefore cannot be considered beautiful.

But isn't beauty "in the eye of the beholder"? This is certainly the common phrase that has reached the level of a cliché. And under this view can't one claim "in the eyes of some beholders, Hitler's life was beautiful"? Certainly one could claim this, but that would not, by itself, make it true. Sometimes clichés reveal truths. Sometimes they reveal falsehoods. The cliché "beauty is in the eye of the beholder" leads to a kind of obstinate subjectivism, which implies that anything at all could be seen as beautiful under certain perspectives (even Hitler's life). But it seems that in this case we could fall prey to the same mistakes as relativism (indeed, subjectivism is simply relativism on the individual scale) and beauty would lose its meaning. If beauty were in the eye of the beholder, for example, a smudge of mud on a canvas could arguably be as beautiful as Michelangelo's "David," for those who fancy the smudge of mud. But I think that we all can readily see that this is an absurdity, and that anyone who wishes to defend the smudge of mud over Michelangelo's work is either in great need of improvement in eyesight or judgment, or perhaps is just being obstinate for its own sake.

Within the reasoning of Aristotle and Moore, we see that beauty is not dependent on the beholder; beauty is dependent on truth (since it requires harmony and balance) and goodness (since anything evil is ugly, not beautiful). The dependence of beauty on truth as a kind of harmony is discussed by Aristotle who says in the Poetics that "to be beautiful, a living creature, and every whole made up of parts, must ... present a certain order in its arrangement of parts."[38] This dependence of beauty on goodness is explained by G.E. Moore who tells us that "To say that a thing is beautiful is to say, not indeed that it is itself good, but that it is a necessary element in something which is: to prove that a thing is truly beautiful is to prove that a whole, to which it bears a particular relation as a part, is truly good."[39] According to this view, then, something or someone is "truly beautiful" in so far as they have harmony and dependence on what is "truly good."

With this insight we have arrived at an important place, since in it all three of our key values are connected: *Beauty* depends on *Goodness* to be *True*. In this way the Platonic conception of the inter-relationship between these key values is supported in Aristotle and Moore. And in speaking of "true beauty," of course, the possibility of "false beauty" arises. It seems that we can surmise that false beauty is detached from truth and divorced from goodness.

There are those, however, who oppose this Platonic conception of beauty and for them phrases like "false beauty," are meaningless, and the requirement that beauty be connected to good is misguided. This view is known as "Aestheticism" and argues that beauty has its own distinct values that cannot and should not be subordinated to other values such as truth and goodness. Regarding what those values are, aestheticism aligns itself with subjectivism since it argues that art is primarily the creation of the individual artist, and is therefore defined by the artist, and not be anything outside their art. It has also been called "art for art's sake" indicating that art or beauty is its own end and should not be evaluated by values such as truth and goodness.

One of the champions of this view was Oscar Wilde, the brilliant 19th century Irish playwright and novelist. For Wilde there is no such thing as "false beauty," since art has its own truth, and there is no such thing as "immoral art" because art should not be judged by the standards of morality. Wilde states this view clearly in his masterpiece *The Picture of Dorian Gray*. "There is no such thing as an immoral book," he writes in the preface, "a book is either well written or poorly written, that is all."[40]

We should note that from the beginning the term "aesthetic" has been tied to sensory experiences. In particular it refers to the feeling of pleasure one has while experiencing beauty. In this way beauty has ties to the physical sensations in a way that truth and goodness do not. What is intriguing, however, is that Wilde—the champion of "aestheticism"—has his character Dorian being poisoned by a work of art (a mysterious "Yellow Book") in his novel. The Yellow Book, which is given to him by Lord Henry (who serves as a bad influence on Dorian throughout the novel), instructs Dorian in a lifestyle filled with immoderate and excessive aestheticism. A life, that is, of debauchery and lasciviousness where selfish pleasure is the goal. Wilde's novel, then, provides a warning against the decadence that can result from such unlimited hedonism. In this fascinating novel, Dorian trades in his soul to remain forever young and physically beautiful. In doing so, however, his soul decays from within. His heart and actions become very ugly and evil, leading even to murder. In the end Dorian falls prey to his desire for a beauty that is removed from truth and goodness.

Within Wilde's masterpiece we seem to find an inherent contradiction within aestheticism. Again, aestheticism claims that no values outside artistic ones should be used to judge it. But *The Picture of Dorian Gray* is a beautiful work of art itself, and as such it is an exquisite critique of the excesses of aestheticism. These excesses are the excesses of hedonism. And it is important to note that a central message of this book is that hedonism cannot provide the true and good "end" we all seek. It fails to be the goal of human living. It cannot be the "good we seek," as Aristotle puts it. Hedonism is what happens when the pleasures experienced within beauty are taken too far. That is was Dorian's mistake. It is also the mistake of aestheticism itself.

We should note here that an interesting comparison could be made between the three anti-Platonic views on truth, beauty, and goodness: namely, formalism, aestheticism and relativism. Each of them claim that their values are simply human creations created in a closed system, whereby the values within each refer only to each other and cannot and should not be tied to or evaluated by anything outside them. Truth, as formalism sees it, belongs simply to the formulas themselves that we humans create, and there is no sense of "truth" outside the formal system itself. Beauty, according to aestheticism, similarly argues that beauty is created by the human mind ("in the eye of the beholder") and that its values cannot be judged in relationship to values outside the system of aesthetics, such as truth and goodness. Goodness, as seen within relativism, also claims that goodness is created by the human mind, since it is merely the system of choices made within cultures, and should not be judged by standards outside those cultural systems. It seems that each provides a similar case. It also seems that each leaves out something of great importance. In formalism, truth has no connection to beauty and goodness. In aestheticism, beauty is separated from truth and goodness. In relativism, goodness is divorced from truth and beauty.

We have seen the problems inherent in each. Formalism has the problems of incompleteness and of the "unreasonable effectiveness." Aestheticism has the problems of subjectivism and excessive hedonism. Relativism has the problems of self-refutation and contradiction. Given the problems inherent in each, we seem to arrive at further support for the Platonic view. Within Platonism Truth, Beauty, and Goodness are not divorced from each other and have independent reality outside of the systems created by human minds.

As we draw this conversation to a close it is important to note that we have barely scratched the surface. So much more could be said. So much more *needs* to be said. I will mention only two areas that I believe would provide useful exploration. First, and as we have seen, Plato described the healthy mind as a balance between reason, spirit and appetite. These seem to link up nicely with our key values: reason to Truth, spirit to Goodness, and appetite to Beauty. In this way the human mind seems uniquely fitted to the pursuit of a meaningful life which must be guided by those key values. Secondly, I will note that Aristotle's doctrine of the "Golden Mean" within his theory of ethics also provides valuable insight into the relationship between truth, beauty and goodness. As we have seen, truth and beauty are tied to harmony, balance, and symmetry. For Aristotle goodness is a balance too, since true virtue, he argued, always lies as a mean between extremes. The virtue of wisdom, for example, lies in the mean between ignorance and arrogance, courage between cowardice and reckless or rash behavior, temperance between anorexia and gluttony, etc. [41]

We should also note that 150 years or so before Aristotle these concepts were taught within Confucius's doctrine of the "Golden Mean" and the Buddha's Deer Park Sermon on the great "Middle Path." [42] In considering these things it seems that we have put our finger on an essential connection between truth, beauty, and goodness—namely, all three exhibit the qualities of balance and harmony.

NOTES

1. Albert Einstein's quote was retrieved on 9/10/15 from: http://www.quotationspage.com/quote/5077.html.

2. Aristotle, *Physics*, in Richard McKeon, trans. *The Basic Works of Aristotle* (New York: Random House, 1941), 184a10–21.

3. Aristotle, *Posterior Analytics*, in Richard McKeon, 72b 19-24.

4. G.E. Moore, *Principia Ethica* (Cambridge: Cambridge University Press, 1903), Chapter 6.

5. For Moore's views see "Intuitionism in Ethics," *Stanford Encyclopedia of Philosophy*. http://plato.stanford.edu/entries/intuitionism-ethics/

6. For more on Parmenides, see G.S. Kirk and J.E. Raven, *The Presocratic Philosophers* (Cambridge: Cambridge University Press, 1975), Chapter 10.

7. Werner Heisenberg, as quoted in the New York Times Book Review (March 8, 1992), found on 9/10/15 at http://izquotes.com/quote/236412

8. Roger Penrose, *The Emperor's New Mind*: (New York: Oxford University Press, 1989), and *The Road to Reality: A Complete Guide to the Laws of the Universe* (London: Random House, 2004). For more on Penrose's views, see his interview with Karl Giberson retrieved on 9/10/15: http://quantum.webhost.uits.arizona.edu/prod/sites/default/files/The%20Man%20Who%20Fell%20to%20Earth.pdf

9. For a discussion on mathematical Platonism, see Phillip Davis and Reuben Hersh, *The Mathematical Experience*, (Boston: Houghton Mifflin, 1981).

10. For Rene Thom's Platonism and that of others see the following retrieved on 9/10/15 at: http://faculty.fordham.edu/klima/phil180/PlatoinMath.html. For the Quine/Putnam thesis: See Stanford Encyclopedia of Philosophy, http://plato.stanford.edu/entries/mathphil-indis/

11. Ibid.

12. Kurt Gödel, as quoted in Phillip Davis and Reuben Hersh, *The Mathematical Experience*, (Boston: Houghton Mifflin, 1981), 319. 7. For more on Gödel's importance in the history of mathematics and logic see Martin Davis, *Engines of Logic: Mathematicians and the Origin of the Computer* (New York: W. W. Norton, 2000), chapter 6. For more on his Platonism, see "Gödel's Platonism" discussed in "Philosophy of Mathematics," *Stanford Encyclopedia of Philosophy*: http://plato.stanford.edu/entries/philosophy-mathematics/.

13. Wigner, E. P. "The unreasonable effectiveness of mathematics in the natural sciences." Richard Courant lecture in mathematical sciences, delivered at New York University, May 11, 1959. For more on the debate between Platonism and Formalism see these websites accessed on 9/10/15: https://www.youtube.com/watch?v=S2YfEXOwpz0, and https://www.youtube.com/watch?v=HHMKnwCT_Dk

14. Benoit Mandlebrot TED Talk: "Fractals and the Art of Roughness," (2010) http://www.ted.com/talks/benoit_mandelbrot_fractals_the_art_of_roughness?language=en. Also of

interest is the Big Think Interview with Mandlebrot: https://www.youtube.com/watch?v=Xm-2ouPGrlY

15. The quote from Ralph Waldo Emerson is from his essay "Beauty" published in his book "Nature" and can be retrieved at http://emersoncentral.com/beauty.htm.

16. John Keats' poem "Ode to a Grecian Urn," can be retrieved at: http://www.poe tryfoundation.org/poem/173742.

17. Emily Dickinson's poem can be retrieved at: http://www.online-literature.com/dickinson/445/.

18. Plato, *Meno*, in Hamilton, Edith and Cairns, Huntington, trans., *The Collected Dialogues of Plato* (New Jersey: Princeton University Press, 1961), 84a-85d.

19. For Penrose's view on Mandelbrot's set see: http://www.dhushara.com/book/quantcos/penrose/penr.htm.

20. For Mandlebrot's discussion of this, see Arthur C. Clark's wonderful documentary available on youtube at: https://www.youtube.com/results?search_query=Arthur +C.+Clark +Mandlebrot.

21. For a discussion of C. J. Jung on "Mandalas" see: http://jungcurrents.com/carl-jung-ten-quotations-about-mandalas.

22. Aristotle, *Metaphysics*, in Richard McKeon, trans., *The Basic Works of Aristotle* (New York: Random House, 1941), 1078a 33-1078b.

23. According to historians of mathematics, the Babylonians discovered the theorem even before Pythagoras and the Chinese did so independently. Listen to the discussion retrieved on 9/10/15 at: http://www.bbc.co.uk/programmes/p0054799

24. Mario Livio, *The Golden Ratio: The Story of the World's Most Astonishing Number* (New York: Broadway Books, 2002).

25. Ibid.

26. Bertrand Russell, *The Study of Mathematics* (Longman, 1919), 60.

27. Paul Erdős, as quoted in Keith Devlin, *Do Mathematicians Have Different Brains?* (New York: Basic Books, 2000), 140.

28. Paul Dirac, as quoted in Subrahmanyan Chandrasekhar, *Truth and Beauty: Aesthetics and Motivations in Science* (Chicago: University of Chicago Press, 1990), 148.

29. Ibid.

30. For a comprehensive summary of theories of truth within philosophy, see "Truth": Stanford Encyclopedia of Philosophy at: http://plato.stanford.edu/entries/truth/

31. See P.N. Furbank's "Thomas Nagel's Mind and Cosmos." *The Threepenny Review* (2012), available at: https://www.threepennyreview.com/samples/jonesfurbank_f12.html

32. Plato, *The Republic*, in Hamilton and Cairns, Huntington, 508e2-3.

33. Einstein quote retrieved on 9/10/15 from: http://www.sfheart.com/einstein.html. Also see Robert N. Goldman, *Einstein's God—Albert Einstein's Quest as a Scientist and as a Jew to Replace a Forsaken God* (Northvale, New Jersey: Joyce Aronson Inc., 1997), 88.

34. Ibid.

35. Einstein's quotes on Gandhi can be retrieved from: http://streams.gandhiserve.org/einstein.html

36. Gandhi's views on truth are found at: http://gandhi-manibhavan.org/gandhiphilosophy/philosophy_truth_meaning.htm

37. For more on Einstein's thoughts on Gandhi see: http://streams.gandhiserve.org/einstein.html.

38. Aristotle, *Poetics*, in Richard McKeon, 1450b-34.

39. G. E. Moore, *Principia Ethica* (Cambridge: Cambridge University Press, 1903), 201.

40. Oscar Wilde, *The Picture of Dorian Gray* (New York, Penguin Classics, 1890), preface. For a discussion on Oscar Wilde's aestheticism, see the article on "Aestheticism and Morality," found at: http://www.bu.edu/writingprogram/journal/past-issues/issue-1/duggan/.

41. For more on Aristotle's "Doctrine of the Mean" see the entry in Stanford Encyclopedia of Philosophy available at: http://plato.stanford.edu/entries/aristotle-ethics/

42. For more on these ideas found Confucius and The Buddha, see David S. Noss and Blake R. Grangaard, *History of the World's Religions* (New York: Pearson Publishing, 2012), Chapters 6 and 8.

Chapter Eight

The Wild Longing of the Human Heart

The title for this text borrows directly from *The Myth of Sisyphus*, a seminal work by the 20th century French-Algerian playwright, novelist, and existential philosopher Albert Camus. There he speaks of the "wild longing for clarity whose call echoes in the human heart."[1] For him it is a yearning and a hope to encounter a world of rationality, purpose, and meaning. For Camus however, this hope is dashed since he believed that the universe is "absurd"—meaning it is just there, it is not rational, it is devoid of purpose, in short, the universe does not respond to our call for communication. Camus further explains:[2]

> The absurd is born of this confrontation between the human need and the unreasonable silence of the world. This must not be forgotten . . . The irrational, the human nostalgia and the absurd which is born of their encounter—these are the three characters of the drama . . .

He believed, however, that even within an absurd universe we could still create a meaningful life by "revolting" and "rebelling" against injustices inherent in the human condition. For him the causes were many: anti-war, anti-discrimination, anti-capital punishment, and resistance to all forms of oppression. His defining moment came when he joined the French Resistance Movement and published an underground newspaper protesting the Nazi occupation of France.

The Myth of Sisyphus is an important work within the existential tradition in philosophy, and along with his other works earned Camus the Nobel Prize for literature awarded "for his important literary production, which with clear-sighted earnestness illuminates the problems of the human conscience in our times."[3] Fittingly in his acceptance speech Camus stated that what motivated his literary work was "two commitments," namely "the refusal to lie about what one knows and the resistance to oppression."[4]

Camus' position in *Sisyphus*—that the universe is ultimately absurd—is not arrived at through some incontrovertible empirical evidence given nor is it the result of some deductively certain argumentation. This is not the style of the existentialist writer in any case. Camus' position, rather, is his judgment, his deeply felt conviction. It all comes down to his personal verdict on the universe. Others, of course, agree with this verdict. In "A Free Man's Worship," logician Bertrand Russell famously makes a similar case:[5]

> Such, in outline, but even more purposeless, more void of meaning, is the world which Science presents for our belief. Amid such a world, if anywhere, our ideals henceforward must find a home. That Man is the product of causes which had no prevision of the end they were achieving; that his origin, his growth, his hopes and fears, his loves and his beliefs, are but the outcome of accidental collocations of atoms; that no fire, no heroism, no intensity of thought and feeling, can preserve an individual life beyond the grave; that all the labours of the ages, all the devotion, all the inspiration, all the noonday brightness of human genius, are destined to extinction in the vast death of the solar system, and that the whole temple of Man's achievement must inevitably be buried beneath the debris of a universe in ruins—all these things, if not quite beyond dispute, are yet so nearly certain, that no philosophy which rejects them can hope to stand. Only within the scaffolding of these truths, only on the firm foundation of unyielding despair, can the soul's habitation henceforth be safely built.

Russell was one of the greatest logicians of his day. However, his verdict on the universe is not the result of undeniable evidence or irrefutable argumentation any more than Camus'. If it were, any opposing argument would be logically invalid and unacceptable. However, Kurt Gödel (as we have seen is called "the greatest logician since Aristotle") disagrees with Russell's verdict and was convinced that the universe is rational and orderly.[6] And if Russell were correct that a "purposeless" universe and one "void of meaning," is the *only* view that "science presents for our belief," then it would not be possible for scientists to disagree with him. However, Albert Einstein (the greatest scientist of the 20th century and perhaps since Isaac Newton) does very much disagree. His often revisited remarks that "God does not play dice with the universe" and "I believe in Spinoza's God," reflect his firm conviction and belief in the rational and ordered nature of the universe.[7]

Gödel and Einstein were close friends as well as colleagues. Both were refugees of Hitler's Germany and came at the end of their careers to Princeton's Institute for Advanced Studies. Einstein often remarked that he enjoyed going to work each day "just to have the privilege to walk home and converse with Gödel."[8] Einstein was recognized worldwide, of course, for his grand theories on relativity that showed science how to view the universe is an entirely different way. Though he provided Einstein with important mathematical proofs for some of his work on the relativity of space-time, Gödel is less well known except by philosophers, mathematicians, and physicists. As we have seen he is known mainly for his work completed in his mid-twenties (roughly the same age as Camus when he penned *The Myth of Sisyphus*) resulting in his famous "Incompleteness Theorems" which are considered the greatest advance in logic since Aristotle, and one of the most important advances in mathematical history. As we have noted, the incompleteness theorems show that every formal system of truth is incomplete in the sense that there will be truths that are not provable within it. This sent shock waves through the logical and mathematical worlds. Most had believed that with enough work and time all true statements or formulas could eventually be proven—as we saw, this was the project of mathematician David Hilbert—but Gödel proved otherwise. In short, there are things we know to be true that cannot be proven.

This insight is relevant by way of analogy for our discussion here concerning which verdict on the universe is correct. Taking our lead from Gödel's theorem we can argue that neither verdict is provable. We are forced, therefore, to choose. We must take our position. Our verdict must be based on our own convictions. This means that the existentialists are right—beginning with Søren Kierkegaard—namely, the most important questions in life are not a matter of provable knowledge, rather, they involve the "either/or" and we all must choose.

Again, though he refers to his verdict as "my reasoning," Camus' words do not form an argument for the absurd:[9]

> My reasoning wants to be faithful to the evidence that aroused it. That evidence is the absurd. It is that divorce between the mind that desires and the world that disappoints, my nostalgia for unity, this fragmented universe and the contradiction that binds them together."

But this is not "reasoning" in the normal sense, which requires logical demonstration or empirical evidence. The absurd cannot be the evidence for itself, except within an unacceptable and fallacious form of circular reasoning. In fact for Camus the absurd is not really a result of argumentation because it is not a "result" at all—it is his beginning. He admits as much when he writes: "The absurd is the essential concept and the first truth," and "The realization that life is absurd cannot be an end, but only a beginning. This is a truth nearly all great minds have taken as their starting point."[10] Once again we see that the absurd is not a position arrived at via reasoning, demonstration or evidence, rather, it is Camus' beginning point, it is his verdict.

Furthermore "reasoning" requires fair and open-mindedness towards those who disagree with one's position, and as we have seen there are other "great minds" that do not take the absurd as their starting point at all. Camus goes on the attack against those who hold this contrary position and accuses them of "philosophical suicide." In particular he cites Kierkegaard, Jaspers, Chestov—all of whom he rejects for their religious verdicts, and Husserl—who he rejects because "he sounds like Plato."[11]

So we are confronted with Camus' verdict. What else can be said? Either you agree with him that the universe is absurd (and therefore the wild longing comes to nothing), or you do not. How can we move forward? We can only do so by comparing opposing verdicts and measuring them to the extent that we can, then each of us must choose our own verdicts. I propose that we compare the verdict of Camus with that of his fellow French existentialist Gabriel Marcel. The two provide stark contrast. Camus sees "despair" and looming "alienation" leading to what he claims is the only "truly serious philosophical problem, and that is suicide."[12] Marcel finds "hope" and the possibility of "participation" in and "with" the wonderful "Mystery of Being" wherein "love is the only starting point."[13] Camus speaks of "the unreasonable silence of the world."[14] Marcel speaks of a "reality [which] *is* on my side," and of his belief that "at the heart of being," there is a "mysterious principle which is in connivance with me."[15]

Both describe the wild longing as an "appeal." Camus speaks of *l'appel humaine*—the human appeal; Marcel speaks of "ontological exigence"—the need for being. Camus' verdict is that the appeal is absurd because the universe remains silent in the face of it. Marcel, on the other hand, sees the appeal itself as an "interior urge" which is already a rudimentary form of communication in and with the universe:[16]

> Being is—or should be—necessary. It is impossible that everything should be reduced to a play of successive appearances that are inconsistent with each other... or, in the words of Shakespeare, to 'a tale told by an idiot.' I aspire to participate in this being, in this reality—and perhaps this aspiration is already a degree of participation, however rudimentary.

Their verdicts, therefore, cannot be more different. How shall we measure them? As we have seen Camus' "reasoning" is like a dog chasing its tail: the absurd is its own evidence. Marcel, on the other hand, goes on the offensive and provides an argument against the verdict of the absurd. In challenging the absurd Marcel does not directly confront Camus but, rather, his colleague Jean Paul Sartre who also embraces the absurd in his novel *Nausea* and in his monumental treatise *Being and Nothingness* where he writes "It is absurd that we are born, it is absurd that we die."[17] And Sartre agreed with Camus' that the absurd ensures that there can be no objective basis for values or any sense of an objective meaning of life. "Belief in the meaning of life," Camus tells us, "always implies a scale of values, a choice, our preference. Belief in the absurd, according to our definitions, teachings the contrary."[18] In an absurd universe, values can have no reality outside of the individuals and cultures that choose them.

What are the values chosen by Camus and Sartre? Both were courageous men who believed in defending justice against injustices, and they risked much (even their very lives) by rebelling against the Nazi occupation of France and joining the Resistance. In doing so they deserve our greatest respect and admiration for their bravery in the face of the evils of Hitler's regime. The values they chose reflected courage in the face of those injustices.

But is it proper to speak of the values they "chose"? For Marcel there is a central flaw in thinking that values are chosen. On the contrary he believed "that 'value' is essentially something which cannot be chosen."[19] "I find that I do not 'choose' my values at all," he writes, "but that I recognize them."[20] What is Marcel's argument here? In particular he challenges the consistency of Sartre's views (and by extension, those of Camus) that values are chosen:[21]

> Now I ask you in the name of what principle, having first denied the existence of values or at least of their objective basis, can he establish any appreciable difference between those utterly misguided but undoubtedly courageous men who joined voluntarily the Anti-Bolshevik Legion, on the one hand, and the heroes of the Resistance movement on the other? I see no way of establishing the difference without admitting that causes have their intrinsic value and, consequently, that values are real.

Again, Marcel's critique here is directed at Sartre personally. In speaking of the Bolshevik Legion, Marcel refers to something that eventually drove Camus and Sartre apart. Sartre was optimistic about communism as it was developing in the Soviet Union since the Bolshevik revolution, while Camus rejected the injustices of the concentration camps discovered there. In any case, Marcel's critique can be restated as follows: in an absurd universe, where values have no objective basis, we cannot consistently maintain that "justice" is only on the side of those who resisted the Nazis. Against the backdrop of the absurd, there is no standard, no measuring stick and, in the words of Friedrich Nietzsche who is the forbearer of the absurd, there is no more "up or down."[22] As such, we have no objective basis to applaud the members of the Resistance as opposed to the Nazis. But Camus and Sartre *do* want to maintain that Nazism represents a form of oppression and evil, and that justice is found in the Resistance. Therein lies the inconsistency. Marcel is offering us a long recognized form of reasoning known as the *modus tollens,* which has the following form: If X implies Y, and Y is false, then X is also false. In short, Marcel's point is as follows: if the absurd is true, then the Nazi's position would be as just as the Resistance fighter's (since there is no objective basis to decide otherwise); but Nazism is not as just, therefore the absurd is false.

As we have seen, we should admire Camus for his bravery in the face of the injustices of Nazism. Marcel's point is that we can only admire him by rejecting the absurd and embracing an objective basis for value—*values which we recognize rather than choose.* In the face of those values we choose and are defined by our choices. We act in recognition of the principles of justice or we do not. If we are to live just lives, we are bound to those principles. But if the absurd is true there are no principles of justice other than those we choose. But our opponents can choose their principles, too (which will be the opposite of ours) and call them "just" too. In this case the word "justice" ceases to have any meaning that we can be bound to. In such a world, the Resistance fighter is in no more "just" position than the Nazi. And in such a world, Camus will not be able to live up to his "two commitments: the refusal to lie about what one knows and the resistance to oppression," because "lies" will can have no meaning in a world where truths are simply chosen rather than recognized, and "oppression" will simply be the futile claims from those who happen to be on the losing end in an absurd world— which feels no duty to respond, thereby ignoring them.

But can we not admire Camus simply for his "authenticity"? It is the existential philosophers who introduce us to authenticity as a kind of personal truth, beginning with Kierkegaard who once stated it clearly: "The thing is to find a truth which is true for me, . . . the idea for which I can live and die . . ."[23] Our admirations for authenticity are reinforced in Shakespeare's words, too: "This above all: to thine own self be true . . ."[24] But there are requirements for authenticity; it cannot stand on its own. It cannot simply be following "one's own truth," or "remaining true to oneself." If it were there would be no reason to admire it. Hitler could be said to have achieved authenticity as much as Gandhi since they both, after all, aligned themselves to a goal and an "idea for which they can live and die." No. We admire authenticity only when it includes a reference point to something outside of the self, the subject who chooses. We admire Camus not because he was simply "true to himself," (as even the Nazi can be). We admire him because he was true to the principles of justice that are real and exist outside of the self who lives according to them. We admire Camus because he fought bravely against injustice. But as we have seen, within the backdrop of the absurd justice has no foothold since, as Camus himself points out, within the absurd "there is no scale of values." In praising Camus, therefore, we must reject the absurd, and in rejecting the absurd we embrace its opposite: a world of truth, beauty and goodness.

It is interesting to note here that what we can call "absurdism" shares the same fault we discovered within formalism, aestheticism, and relativism. Namely, it is bound up within itself and cannot escape its own system. It cannot provide any foundation for evaluation outside itself. But in order to praise the Resistance fighter over the Nazi, we must refer to values outside the absurd system.

Marcel shows us the inconsistency of Camus' absurdism. With Marcel we see that we should focus on the wild longing itself, the "nostalgia for unity" (as Camus puts it), rather than the absurd, which is Camus' verdict on that fact. Again, the absurd cannot be its own evidence. The wild longing, on the other hand, is its own evidence—for it is felt in the human heart and it is inherent in the human condition. The wild longing is the basic fact. We feel it within ourselves, and we see it as the main motivation for all human activity—art, philosophy and science—in all cultures. Carl Jung recognizes it as "this 'call of the wild,' the longing for fulfillment," which "if you can prove receptive" to it "will quicken the sterile wilderness of your soul as rain quickens dry earth."[25] For Jung the wild longing flows from the Collective Unconscious we all share in, and are revealed in the myths and stories from all cultures around the world. Inspired by Jung, Joseph Campbell found that within each myth the wild longing reveals the same story—the "monomyth" (a term he borrows from James Joyce) as revealed in "the hero's journey." Each culture and each individual goes through the same journey and struggles, thus Campbell refers to the "hero with a thousand faces" presented in the mythic stories and artwork from ancient societies to the present day.[26]

Though it is found everywhere, the wild longing has a special and central place in German culture where it is called "*Sehnsucht*," referring to a clear, though not completely definable longing or yearning after something which is remote and not quite completely attainable, but which nevertheless pulls us towards it.[27] Incidentally, Marcel recognizes this as well when he describes the wild longing as "a straining oneself towards something, as when, for instance, during the night we attempt to get a distinct perception of some far-off noise."[28] For the medieval and fabled German poet Heinrich Von Ofterdingen, it is symbolized as a perfect and mysterious blue flower that we all "yearn to get a glimpse of . . ."[29] The Blue Flower (*Blaue Blume*) became a central symbol in literature, standing for the longing after the infinite and unattainable. It has been widely used by, among many others, Novalis, Goethe, Henry Van Dyke, Emily Dickinson, Walter Benjamin and Tennessee Williams. C. S. Lewis remarks in his *Surprised by Joy* that he is "a votary of the Blue Flower" and connects it to the German *Sehnsucht*.[30] Lewis discusses it also in his *The Pilgrim's Regress*, describing it as an "inconsolable longing" in the human heart for "that unnamable something" a something "we know not what."[31] "*Sensucht*" is so central a concept to Lewis that it is the title of the current journal devoted to his work.[32]

The wild longing (*Sehnsucht*) is also that which drives all British Romantic poetry as well. It is the source of what Wordsworth called in his preface to the *Lyrical Ballads*, "the spontaneous overflow of powerful feelings." It is that which he expresses in his "Tintern Abbey" poem, as:[33]

> The still, sad music of humanity, / A presence that disturbs me with the joy / Of elevated thoughts; a sense sublime / Of something far more deeply infused, / Whose dwelling is in the light of the setting suns, / And the round ocean and the living air, / And the blue sky, and in the mind of man: / A motion and a spirit, that impels / All thinking things and all objects of thought, / And rolls through all things / ... The anchor of my purest thoughts, the nurse, / The guide, the guardian of my heart, and soul / Of all my moral being . . . ."

It is also what Keats describes in his "Ode to a Nightingale":[34]

> My heart aches, and a drowsy numbness pains / . . . The voice I hear this passing night was heard / In ancient days by emperor and clown:/ Perhaps the self-same song that found a path / Through the sad heart of Ruth, when, sick for home, / She stood in tears amid the alien corn; / The same oft-times hath / Charm'd magic casements, opening on the foam / Of perilous seas, in faery lands forlorn. / Forlorn! The very word is like a bell / To toll me back from thee to my sole self!

The German artist Oskar Zwintscher offers a hauntingly beautiful example of *Sehnsucht* in his painting of the same name, which has been described as the feeling of something "intensely missing . . . sometimes felt as a longing for a far-off country, but not a particular earthly land we can identify. Furthermore there is something in the experience that suggests this far-off country is very familiar and indicative of what we might otherwise call 'home.' In this sense it is a type of 'Nostalgia,' in the original sense of that word."[35] And for German poet A.W. Schlegel all works of art are an expression of *Sehnsucht* seen as a longing and craving after some feeling of unity previously felt by us all.[36] These last notions tie in perfectly with Camus' description of the wild longing as our "nostalgia for unity."[37]

The notion of "nostalgia" should be examined more closely. The word derives from the Greek root "nostos" (to return home), so refers to a kind of "homesickness" (think of Keats' reference to Ruth's being "sick for home"). The wild longing contains the nostalgia within it. Interestingly, we have seen that the postmodernist thinkers, Lyotard in particular, argue that the search for "the truth" is tied to "our nostalgia for the whole and the one" which we need to abandon. And Camus agrees, saying that the absurd man recognizes that "His exile is without remedy since he is deprived of the memory of a lost home . . ."[38]

In urging us to abandon it postmodernism and Camus admit to the presence of this feeling of nostalgia and homesickness within the wild longing.

How can we explain this feeling? For Kierkegaard the wild longing is linked with the feeling of dread that, he says, "is the only proof of our heterogeneity. For if we lacked nothing . . . no homesickness would attack us."[39] Kierkegaard's reference to heterogeneity suggests a feeling of difference, dissimilarity and strangeness—interestingly, Camus also recognizes the "strangeness of the world."[40] This estrangement reflects our understanding of the difference between the world we live in (this earthly realm) and the world of our wild longing and the source of our homesickness (the world that somehow transcends this earthly realm). We are brought, then, to notion of the wild longing as an appeal towards transcendence.

Camus rejects transcendence and sees the appeal for it as absurd. Marcel, as we have seen, believed that the wild longing itself—the human appeal—is already a rudimentary form of participation in transcendence. For him the nostalgia itself is a response to a signal from the very world we are homesick for. This is very similar to the thought of C. S. Lewis:[41]

> Our lifelong nostalgia, our longing to be reunited with something in the universe from which we now feel cut off, to be on the inside of some door which we have always seen from the outside, is no mere neurotic fancy, but the truest index of our real situation. And to be at last summoned inside would be both glory and honour beyond all our merits and also the healing of that old ache.

For Lewis the feeling of *sensucht* is itself some evidence of the meaning it seeks in the universe: "If the whole universe has no meaning, we should never have found out that it has no meaning: just as, if there were no light in the universe and therefore no creatures with eyes, we should never know it was dark. Dark would be without meaning."[42] Lewis' point seems to be that since we have eyes and seek to see, there must be light to make our vision possible; i.e., the universe must not be dark. In a dark universe eyes would have no purpose. By analogy he is saying that because we have a desire for meaning (*sensucht*), this serves as an important sign that the universe must not be absurd, since if it were, there would be no desire for it not to be absurd. In short, Camus is mistaken: the absurd is not evidence of itself, it is evidence of its opposite.

The focus on the metaphor of light is of interest here. The Sun is the source of light in the physical realm and it was Plato who chose the "Sun" as the symbol for the "Form of the Good," and it is Platonism, as we have seen, that defends belief in the "light" of truth, beauty and goodness. He also defends the innate truth of the wild longing after them. In his famous "Allegory of the Cave" Plato argues that many people remain in a "cave" of darkness and shadows deprived of the "light of the truth" which can only be found outside the cave in the fullness of "light" coming from the "Sun." The

"cave" is our earthly existence; the "Sun" represents truth, beauty, and goodness, which lie outside the cave within a realm that transcends it.[43]

Camus rejects Platonism. We saw this in his criticism of Husserl. His
anti-Platonism is also unmistakable when he writes: "There is no sun without
shadow, and it is essential to know the night."[44] This should be seen as a
direct response to Plato's message within the allegory of the cave. For Camus
the cave represents the reality of our earthly existence that we cannot escape.
The fact that we cannot escape the cave is, for him, what makes the wild
longing absurd and hopeless. For Camus the cave is the only world we have
and shadows represent the only truths we can know. Camus turns Platonism
on its head. For Plato there is no truth without the Sun, and it is essential to
know the light; for Camus "there is no sun without shadow, and it is essential
to know the night." For Plato the Sun is Reality and the shadows are illusions, for Camus shadows are the only reality we have. For Plato shadows
are dependent on the Sun and are caused by obstacles placed between the
light and those who search after it. For Camus the sun is in some ways
dependent on the shadows (again "there is no sun without shadow."). Here
Camus is reminiscent of Nietzsche, his philosophical forbearer, whose hero
Zarathustra comes out of the cave and tells the sun: "You great star, what
would your happiness be had you not those for whom you shine?"[45] For
Nietzsche, as for Camus, the sun depends on us, not us on the sun. For both
there is no reality except the reality we create. And as Nietzsche makes clear
we have "unchained the earth from the sun" and are now moving "away from
all suns."[46]

Their message is clear: we do not need the light of Plato's "Sun"—for we
will make our own truth, beauty, and goodness. For Nietzsche, Zarathustra
represents the hero who teaches us to live without suns. For Camus, the hero
is Sisyphus who teaches us how to rebel and revolt against the absurd. In the
Greek myth Sisyphus tricked the gods and cheated death. For this he is
condemned to an absurd punishment of rolling a rock up a mountain only to
watch it roll back down again after reaching the summit. After this he has no
recourse but to walk down the mountain and begin his meaningless task all
over again, forever. Camus likens this to the daily routines that make life
seem meaningless to us. "The workman of today," he writes "works everyday in his life at the same tasks, and his fate is no less absurd."[47] Camus'
words are drearily descriptive: "It happens that the stage sets collapse. Rising, streetcar, four hours in the office or the factory, meal, streetcar, four
hours of work, meal, sleep, and Monday Tuesday Wednesday Thursday Fri-
day and Saturday according to the same rhythm . . ."[48]

Sisyphus' lot seems tragic and without redemption. But Camus thinks he
can be saved. His salvation comes in his revolt and rebellion. For Camus
"Sisyphus is the absurd hero:"[49]

He is, as much through his passions as through his torture. His scorn of the gods, his hatred of death, and his passion for life . . . he is superior to his fate. He is stronger than his rock . . . There is no fate that cannot be surmounted by scorn . . . Happiness and the absurd are two sons of the same earth. They are inseparable . . .

I leave Sisyphus at the foot of the mountain! One always finds one's burden again. But Sisyphus teaches the higher fidelity that negates the gods and raises rocks. He too concludes that all is well. This universe henceforth without a master seems to him neither sterile nor futile. Each atom of that stone, each mineral flake of that night filled mountain, in itself forms a world. The struggle itself toward the heights is enough to fill a man's heart. One must imagine Sisyphus happy.

But can Camus' redemption of Sisyphus succeed? Perhaps we can imagine him happy, though I confess great difficulty in doing so. But we cannot imagine his fate as just nor his life as meaningful. And as our journey in this text has shown, happiness is not the goal of human living in any event. If Sisyphus is happy it is of little consequence, for it occurs only inside his head. It may temporarily prevent him from going mad, but it does not address the injustice of his situation and does not repair it. Thinking that his scorn of the gods matters, when there are no gods to care, is its own kind of madness. The tragedy and injustice of his fate gets no response from a universe that remains unreasonably silent. His struggle may fill his heart, but it cannot quiet its wild longing.

NOTES

1. Albert Camus, The Myth of Sisyphus (New York: Vintage Books, 1955), 16.

2. Ibid.

3. Camus' Nobel Prize Acceptance Speech is available at the following website last retrieved on 9/10/15: http://www.nobelprize.org/nobel_prizes/literature/laureates/1957/

4. Ibid.

5. Bertrand Russell, "A Free Man's Worship" (1903) retrieved on 9/10/15 from: http://www3.nd.edu/~afreddos/courses/264/fmw.htm.

6. For more on Gödel's views see the entry "Kurt Gödel" in the *Stanford Encyclopedia of Philosophy* available at: http://plato.stanford.edu/entries/goedel/

7. Albert Einstein's quote that "God does not play dice" was retrieved on 9/10/15 at: http://www.goodreads.com/author/quotes/9810.Albert_Einstein. Einstein's quote that "I believe in Spinoza's God" is fully explored at: http://www.einsteinandreligion.com/spinoza.html.

8. Einstein's reference to his walks with Gödel is found in Hao Wang, *Reflections on Kurt Gödel* (Boston: MIT Press, 1987), 31.

9. Camus, *The Myth of Sisyphus*, 37.

10. Camus' Review of Sartre's Novel *Nausea*, quoted in Avi Sagi, *Albert Camus and the Philosophy of the Absurd* (Amsterdam: Value Inquiry Book Series, 2002), Vol. 125, 43.

11. Camus, *The Myth of Sisyphus*, 21ff.

12. Ibid., 3.

13. Gabriel Marcel, *The Philosophy of Existentialism*, (Secaucus New Jersey: Citadel Press, 1973), 20.

14. Camus, *The Myth of Sisyphus*, 21.

15. Marcel, *The Philosophy of Existentialism*, PE 28.

16. Marcel, Ibid., 14.

17. Jean Paul Sartre, *Being and Nothingness* (New York: Routledge Press, 1956), 547.

18. Camus, *The Myth of Sisyphus*, 45.

19. Marcel, *Man Against Mass Society* (Chicago: Regnery, 1962).

20. Marcel, *The Philosophy of Existentialism*, 87.

21. Marcel, Ibid., 87.

22. Friedrich Nietzsche, "The Parable of the Madman," in *The Gay Science*, Walter Kaufmann, trans., (New York: Vintage Press, 1974), 181-182. Also see related information retrieved on 9/10/15 from: http://www.historyguide.org/europe/madman.html.

23. Søren Kierkegaard, *A Kierkegaard Anthology,* edited by Robert Bretall, (New York: Modern Library, 1946), Journal entry dated August 1, 1835.

24. William Shakespeare, *Hamlet* Act 1, Scene 3, 78-82.

25. C. G. Jung, *Mysterium Coniunctionis*, Collected Works of C.G. Jung, Volume 14, (Princeton, N.J.: Princeton University Press, 1970), paragraph 190.

26. Joseph Campbell, *The Hero with a Thousand Faces* (New York: Pantheon Books, 1949).

27. For more on the universality of "sensucht," see Susanne Scheibe, et al., "A Cross-Cultural Comparison of Sehnsucht in Germany and the United States," *Developmental Psychology*, 2011, vol., 47, No. 3, 603-618. Also see Susanne Scheibe, Alexandra M. Freund: "Approaching Sehnsucht (Life Longings) from a Life-Span Perspective: The Role of Personal Utopias in Development," *Research in Human Development*, 5 (2), 121–133, 2008.

28. Marcel, *The Mystery of Being, Vol. 1, Reflection and Mystery*, G. S. Fraser, trans., (London: The Harvill Press, 1951), 47.

29. For more on this poet, also known as "Novalis" see the following, retrieved on 9/10/15: http://www.roangelo.net/logwitt/waterman.html

30. C. S. Lewis, *Surprised by Joy* (United Kingdom: Harcourt Brace, 1955), 7.

31. ———, *The Pilgrim's Regress* (United Kingdom: J.M. Dent and Sons, 1933). For more information about Lewis' views on this topic see this website, accessed on 9/10/15: http://www.theimaginativeconservative.org/2013/11/looking-for-another-country-c-s-lewis-and-t-s-eliot.html

32. For reference to the C. S. Lewis Journal "Sehnsucht," see the following website last accessed on 9/10/15: http://www.sehnsucht-cslewis.org/index.html

33. William Wordworth, "Lines Written a Few Miles Above Tintern Abbey," *Lyrical Ballads*, (London: J. & A. Arch, 1798). This poem can be retrieved at this website last accessed on 9/10/15: http://www.rc.umd.edu/sites/default/RCOldSite/www/rchs/reader/tabbey.html

34. John Keats, "Ode to a Nightingale," (1819) was retrieved on 9/10/15 from: http://www.poetryfoundation.org/poem/173744

35. Timothy Keller's discussion of Oskar Zwintscher painting "Sehnsucht," is retrieved at: http://invisiblegazebo.net/sehnsucht/

36. For more information on the German poet A. W. Schlegel, see the article in *The Stanford Encyclopedia of Philosophy* at: http://plato.stanford.edu/entries/schlegel-aw/

37. Camus, *The Myth of Sisyphus,* 37.

38. Ibid., 5.

39. Kierkegaard, *The Concept of Dread* Walter Kaufmann (Princeton: Princeton University Press, 1980), 145, footnote.

40. Camus, *The Myth of Sisyphus*, 11.

41. Lewis, *The Weight of Glory* (New York: The Macmillan Company, 1949). This and other quotes from Lewis can be found at: http://cslewisquotes.tumblr.com/page/10.

42. ———, *Mere Christianity* (New York: Harper Collins, 1952). These and other quotes from lewis are found at http://www.goodreads.com/quotes/tag/c-s-lewis.

43. Plato, *Republic*, in Hamilton, Edith and Cairns, Huntington, trans. *The Collected Dialogues of Plato* (New Jersey: Princeton University Press, 1961), 514a-520a.

44. Camus, *The Myth of Sisyphus*, 91.

45. Nietzsche, *Thus Spake Zarathustra*, Prologue.

46. Friedrich Nietzsche, "The Parable of the Madman," in *The Gay Science,* Walter Kaufmann, trans., (New York: Vintage Press, 1974), Prologue. These lines are also available at: http://www.historyguide.org/europe/madman.html.

47. Camus, *The Myth of Sisyphus*, 90.

48. Ibid., 10.

49. Ibid., 90-91.

Chapter Nine

Conclusion

We began this book contemplating the journey we all take while traveling some 67,000 miles per hour around our sun as it and our entire solar system makes its way around the Milky Way Galaxy—a journey which takes some 250 million years. During the last 1 percent of the most recent journey the universe gave rise to consciousness on that small blue dot of a planet that we call home. That is when our wild longing began. Consciousness and self-awareness marks our distinction. With it we contemplate the universe and ourselves contemplating the universe. As the 17th century French mathematician, physicist and philosopher Blaise Pascal has said, "all our dignity lies in thought."[1]

Our appeal to transcendence, our desire to come to terms with the universe that has granted us consciousness, and the key values that guide us forwards (Truth, Beauty and Goodness), all outline the central mysteries which engage our human journey. These mysteries and our sense of transcendence, as we saw in Marcel, are also reaffirmed in the neuroscientist Ramachandran who connects it to consciousness itself:[2]

> Self-awareness is a trait that not only makes us human but also paradoxically makes us want to be more than merely human. As I said in my BBC Reith Lectures, 'Science tells us we are merely beasts, but we don't feel like that. We feel like angels trapped inside the bodies of beasts, forever craving transcendence.'

We saw that this sense of transcendence is reflected in a feeling of difference and estrangement between us and the physical universe that gave us birth, giving rise to the nostalgia or homesickness that characterizes the wild longing. Pascal recognized both our feebleness and our greatness. "Man is but a reed," he said, "the most feeble thing in nature; but he is a thinking reed," and therein lies our greatness:[3] "A vapor, a drop of water suffices to kill him. But if the universe were to crush him, man would still be more noble that that which killed him, because he knows that he dies and the advantage which the universe has over him; the universe knows nothing of this." What makes us "more noble" than the universe, he thought, is our consciousness. "By space," Pascal continues, "the universe encompasses and swallows me up like an atom; by thought I comprehend the world."[4]

But we cannot comprehend it completely. Pascal was well acquainted with the power of reason since he was one of the greatest mathematicians in history. But he knew that reason, logic, and mathematics could only take us so far, just as Gödel was to later prove. For Pascal what we can understand through reason represents only a fragile sliver of knowledge. It is infinitesimally small in the face of a universe that is infinite. As he explained, "The finite is annihilated in the presence of the infinite, and it becomes a pure nothing,"[5] since it all resides in the finite brains of those fragile reeds that we are. The infinite universe will always maintain, therefore, its mystery. Marcel speaks of this too: "There is an order," he writes, "where the subject finds himself in the presence of something entirely beyond his grasp. I would add that if the word 'transcendent' has any meaning it is here—it designates the absolute, unbridgeable chasm yawning between the subject and being, insofar as being evades every attempt to pin it down."[6]

So we cannot hope in our short human lifetimes to comprehend it all. Somehow in the vastness of space and time the universe was born, perhaps within the death throes of a previous universe. The physical properties of that universe gave rise to heat which in turn gave rise to the elements forged in those vast nuclear furnaces we call stars. All of the elements were created there including all of the atoms that make us up. We are the children of stars. We do not fully understand how it is that simple organisms came to be and how and why they began to make copies of themselves leading to more and more complex forms of existence and life until it led to consciousness. It seems that the universe has its own wild longing.

This fact reveals, perhaps, the greatest mystery of all—namely, that we are *both* different from the universe (in our desire to transcend it) and the *same* as the universe (since we *are* the universe that has become conscious and seeks to understand itself). But though we cannot completely capture this mystery (it, in fact, completely captures us), perhaps we can catch a glimpse of understanding. And if this understanding is not revealed to our reason, perhaps it can be communicated to our hearts. It was Pascal, again, who recognized the difference: "The heart has its reasons, which reason does not know," and "we know truth, not only by the reason, but also by the heart, and it is this last way that we know first principles."[7] And perhaps as we continue to explore the wild longing of the human heart as it seeks those first principles of Truth, Beauty and Goodness, we may also enhance our understanding by remaining open to the inspiration from others who share their glimpse with us. We have seen many glimpses from so many others in this text: the philosophers, mathematicians, logicians, psychologists, poets, and scientists who have enlightened us. And there are more glimpses available to us from the vast array of stories, literature, art, music, and religions from cultures around the world.

These glimpses are available to us all. So many valuable ideas lie waiting there for us to learn from. So many stories await our discovery. They are like precious unwrapped gifts. In Keats' words they are "Charm'd magic casements, opening on the foam, of perilous seas, in faery lands forlorn." Poetically a "magic casement" is a metaphor for a window we can peak through which improves our glimpse of the wonders of life and of the whole universe. As we travel around our Sun at almost unimaginable speeds, we need to take the time to glimpse through those windows—those magic casements—which perhaps reveal to us that other "Sun," in Plato's meaning, which provides the light of Truth, Beauty, and Goodness. Again, we may see them best if we look with our hearts, as Pascal understood. Saint-Exupery said it best in his classic book *The Little Prince*: "Here is my secret," said the fox, "a very simple secret: It is only with the heart that one can see rightly . . ."[8] Our wild longing is, after all, a wild longing of the human heart, so let us see rightly through those magic casements.

There are so many to choose from. Like that true story of the young Indian Prince, who driven by the wild longing renounced his kingdom some 2,500 years ago and set upon his journey. The story of that brave and unrelenting path taken by Siddhartha can help to enlighten us all. Perhaps, if we look rightly, we can learn from his experience as he sat under that Bodhi tree and came to the central realization of his oneness with the universe, thereby arriving home.

NOTES

1. Blaise Pascal, *Pensées*, W. F. Trotter, trans. (New York: Random House, 1941), 116.

2. V. S. Ramachandran, *The Tell-Tale Brain: A Neuroscientist's Quest for What Makes Us Human* (New York: W. W. Norton, 2011). This quote and others from Ramachandran are available at: http://www.goodreads.com/author/quotes/17674.V_S_Ramachandran.

3. Pascal, *Pensées*, 116.

4. Ibid.

5. Ibid., 79.

6. Gabriel Marcel, *Tragic Wisdom and Beyond* (Evanston: Northwestern University Press, 1973), 193.

7. Pascal, *Pensées*, 95.

8. Antoine de Saint-Exupery, *The Little Prince* (New York: Harcourt, 1943), Chapter 21.

Bibliography

Aristotle, *De Anima*, Richard McKeon trans., *The Basic Works of Aristotle* (New York: Random House, 1941).

———, *Metaphysics*, Richard McKeon trans., *The Basic Works of Aristotle* (New York: Random House, 1941).

———, *Nicomachean Ethics*, Richard McKeon trans., *The Basic Works of Aristotle* (New York: Random House, 1941).

———, *Physics*, Richard McKeon trans., *The Basic Works of Aristotle* (New York: Random House, 1941).

———, *Poetics*, Richard McKeon trans. *The Basic Works of Aristotle* (New York: Random House, 1941).

———, *Posterior Analytics*, Richard McKeon trans. *The Basic Works of Aristotle* (New York: Random House, 1941).

Tal Ben-Shahar, *Happier: Learn the Secrets to Daily Joy and lasting Fulfillment* (New York: McGraw Hill, 2007).

Allan Bloom, *The Closing of the American Mind* (New York: Simon and Shuster, 1987).

Franz Boas, "Museums of Ethnology and their Classifications." *Science* 9, (1987).

Jill Bolte. *My Stoke of Insight: A Brain Scientist's Personal Journey* (New York: Viking Press, 2009).

Joseph Campbell, *The Hero with a Thousand Faces* (New York: Pantheon Books, 1949).

Albert Camus, *The Myth of Sisyphus* (New York: Vintage Books, 1955).

Subrahmanyan Chandrasekhar, *Truth and Beauty: Aesthetics and Motivations in Science* (Chicago: University of Chicago Press, 1990), 148.

Mihaly Csikszentmihalyi. *Flow: The Psychology of Optimal Experience* (New York: Harper, 1990).

Martin Davis, *Engines of Logic: Mathematicians and the Origin of the Computer* (New York: W. W. Norton, 2000).

Paul Davies and John Gribbon, *The Matter Myth: Dramatic Discoveries that Challenge Our Understanding of Physical Reality* (New York: Simon and Schuster, 1992).

Phillip Davis and Reuben Hersh, *The Mathematical Experience*, (Boston: Houghton Mifflin, 1981).

Michel deMontaigne, "*Of Experience,*" Charles Cotton, trans., (Paris, 1588).

Jacques Derrida, *Of Grammatology*, Gayatri Chakravorty Spivak, trans., (Baltimore: Johns Hopkins University Press, 1976).

Keith Devlin, *Do Mathematicians Have Different Brains?* (New York: Basic Books, 2000).

Emily Dickinson, "I Died For Beauty," poem #445, printed in Thomas Johnson, *Emily Dickinson, An Interpretative Biography*, (Cambridge: Harvard University Press, 1955).

Denis Diderot and Voltaire, *Encyclopédie* (Paris: Andre le Breton Publisher, 1751–1772).

Umberto Ecco, *The Name of the Rose* (New York: Harcourt, 1983).

Epictetus, *Discourses and Selected Writings*, Robert Dobbin, trans. (London: Penguin Classics, 2008).

Lester Faigley, *Fragments of Rationality: Postmodernity and the Subject of Composition* (Pittsburgh: University of Pittsburgh Press, 1992).

Michel Foucault, "Nietzsche, Genealogy, History," trans., D. Bouchard and S. Sherry, in *Language, Counter-Memory, Practise*, ed. D. Bouchard (Ithaca, N.Y.: Cornell University Press, 1977).

Erich Fromm, *The Art of Loving* (New York: Harper, 1956).

P.N. Furbank: "Thomas Nagel's Mind and Cosmos." *The Threepenny Review* (2012).

Daniel Gilbert, *Stumbling on Happiness* (New York: Vintage Book, 2004).

Robert N. Goldman, *Einstein's God—Albert Einstein's Quest as a Scientist and as a Jew to Replace a Forsaken God* (Northvale, New Jersey: Joyce Aronson Inc., 1997).

W.K.C. Guthrie, *A History of Greek Philosophy* (Cambridge: Cambridge University Press, 1962).

Jûrgen Habermas, *The Philosophical Discourse of Modernity: Twelve lectures* (Cambridge: MIT Press, 1987).

Jonathan Haidt, *The Happiness Hypothesis: Finding Modern Truth in Ancient Wisdom,* (New York: Basic Books, 2006).

Rick Hanson and Richard Mendius, *Buddha's Brain: The Practical Neuroscience of Happiness, Love and Wisdom* (Oakland, CA: New Harbinger Publications, 2009).

Herodotus, *History of the Persian Wars*, translated by David Grene (Chicago: University of Chicago Press, 1985).

Douglas Hofstadter. *Gödel, Escher, Bach: An Eternal Golden Braid* (New York: Basic Books, 1979).

Aldous Huxley, *Brave New World* (United Kingdom: Chatto and Windus, 1932).

C. G. Jung, *The Archetypes and the Collective Unconscious* (London, 1996).

———. *Mysterium Coniunctionis, Collected Works of C.G. Jung*, Volume 14, (Princeton, N.J.: Princeton University Press, 1970).

Daniel Kahneman, *Thinking: Fast and Slow* (New York: Farrar, Straus and Giroux, 2011).

John Keats, "Ode to a Grecian Urn," printed in *The Norton Anthology of English Literature* (3e), (New York: W. W. Norton, 1974).

Søren Kierkegaard, *A Kierkegaard Anthology*, edited by Robert Bretall, (New York: Modern Library, 1946).

———. *The Concept of Dread,* Walter Kaufmann, trans., (Princeton: Princeton University Press, 1980).

G.S. Kirk and J.E. Raven, *The Presocratic Philosophers* (Cambridge: Cambridge University Press, 1975).

Stefan Klein, *The Science of Happiness: How Our Brains Make Us Happy—and What We Can Do to Get Happier* (New York: Marlowe and Company, 2006).

C. S. Lewis, *Mere Christianity* (New York: Harper Collins, 1952).

———. *Surprised by Joy* (United Kingdom: Harcourt Brace, 1955).

———. *The Pilgrim's Regress* (United Kingdom: J.M. Dent and Sons, 1933).

———. *The Weight of Glory* (New York: The Macmillan Company, 1949).

Mario Livio, *The Golden Ratio: The Story of the World's Most Astonishing Number* (New York: Broadway Books, 2002).

Jean-Francois Lyotard, "What is Postmodernism?" in *Art and It's Significance*, Stephen David Ross, editor (New York: State University of New York Press, 1994).

Gabriel Marcel, *Tragic Wisdom and Beyond* (Evanston: Northwestern University Press, 1973).

———. *The Mystery of Being, Vol. 1, Reflection and Mystery*, G. S. Fraser, trans., (London: The Harvill Press, 1951).

———. *The Philosophy of Existentialism*, (Secaucus New Jersey: Citadel Press, 1973).

Karl Marx, "Critique of the Gotha Program" (1875).

Karl Marx and Friedrich Engels, *The Communist Manifesto*, (United Kingdom, 1848).

Abraham Maslow, *Motivation and Personality* (New York: Harper, 1954).

————. *Religions, Values, and Peak Experiences* (London: Penguin Books Limited, 1964).

Paul Mclean, *The Triune Brain in Evolution* (New York: Plenum Press, 1990).

Margaret Mead, *Coming of Age in Samoa* (New York: William Morrow Paperbacks, 1928).

John Stuart Mill, *Utilitarianism* (London: Parker, Son and Bourn, 1863).

G. E. Moore, *Principia Ethica* (Cambridge: Cambridge University Press, 1903).

Thomas Nagel, *Mind and Cosmos: Why the Materialist Neo-Darwinian Conception of Nature Is Almost Certainly False* (Oxford: Oxford University Press, 2012).

Debra Nails, "Socrates," *The Stanford Encyclopedia of Philosophy, 2014.*

J. Nakamura and Mihaly Csikszentmihalyi, *The Concept of Flow* (New York: Oxford University Press, 2005).

Friedrich Nietzsche, "The Parable of the Madman," in *The Gay Science*, Walter Kaufmann, trans., (New York: Vintage Press, 1974).

————. "On Truth and Lies in the Nonmoral Sense," in Walter Kaufmann, trans., *The Portable Nietzsche* (New York: Viking Press, 1960).

David S. Noss and Blake R. Grangaard, *History of the World's Religions* (New York: Pearson Publishing, 2012).

Robert Nozick, *Anarchy, State and Utopia* (New York: Basic Books, 1974).

Blaise Pascal, *Pensées*, W. F. Trotter, trans., (New York: Random House, 1941).

Roger Penrose, *The Emperor's New Mind: Concerning Computers, Minds, and the Laws of Physics* (Oxford: Oxford University Press, 1989).

————. *The Road to Reality: A Complete Guide to the Laws of the Universe* (London: Random House, 2004).

Max Planck, *"Das Wesen der Materie,"* (The Nature of Matter), speech given at Florence, Italy, 1944.

Plato, *Apology*, Edith Hamilton and Huntington Cairns, trans., *The Collected Dialogues of Plato* (New Jersey: Princeton University Press, 1961).

————. *Meno*, Edith Hamilton and Huntington Cairns, trans., *The Collected Dialogues of Plato* (New Jersey: Princeton University Press, 1961).

————. Phaedo, Edith Hamilton and Huntington Cairns, trans., *The Collected Dialogues of Plato* (New Jersey: Princeton University Press, 1961).

————. *Phaedrus,* Edith Hamilton and Huntington Cairns, trans., *The Collected Dialogues of Plato* (New Jersey: Princeton University Press, 1961).

————. *Theatetus,* Edith Hamilton and Huntington Cairns, trans., *The Collected Dialogues of Plato* (New Jersey: Princeton University Press, 1961).

————. *Republic*, Edith Hamilton and Huntington Cairns, trans., *The Collected Dialogues of Plato* (New Jersey: Princeton University Press, 1961).

Louis Pojman, *Introduction to Philosophy* (New York: Oxford University Press, 2004).

Karl Popper, *The Open Society and its Enemies* (London: Routledge & Kegan Paul, 1945).

V. S. Ramachandran, *The Tell-Tale Brain: A Neuroscientist's Quest for What Makes Us Human* (New York: W. W. Norton and Company, 2011).

Brent Dean Robbins, "Positive Psychology and the Renaissance of Humanistic Psychology." *Humanistic Psychologist*, (2008), 36: 96–112.

Carl Rogers, *On Becoming a Person: A Therapist's View of Psychotherapy* (London: Constable, 1961).

Richard Rorty, "Hermeneutics, General Studies and Teaching," printed in *Classic and Contemporary Readings in the Philosophy of Education* (New York: State University of New York Press, 1997).

Jean Jacques Rousseau, *Emile: Treatise on Education*, (Paris: 1762).

Bertrand Russell, *The Study of Mathematics* (Longman, 1919).

————. "A Free Man's Worship," printed in *The Collected Papers of Bertrand Russell, 1902–1914.* (London: Routledge, 1903).

Avi Sagi, *Albert Camus and the Philosophy of the Absurd* (Amsterdam: Value Inquiry Book Series, 2002), Vol. 125.

Jean Paul Sartre, *Being and Nothingness* (New York: Routledge Press, 1956).

Susanne Scheibe, Alexandra M. Freund: "Approaching Sehnsucht (Life Longings) from a Life-Span Perspective: The Role of Personal Utopias in Development." *Research in Human Development*, 5 (2), 121–133, (2008).

Susanne Scheibe, et al., "A Cross-Cultural Comparison of Sehnsucht in Germany and the United States." *Developmental Psychology* vol. 47, No. 3, 603–618, (2011).

Barry Schwartz. *The Paradox of Choice: Why More is Less,* (New York: Harper Collins, 2004).

Martin Seligman, *Authentic Happiness: Using the New Positive Psychology to Realize Your Potential for Lasting Fulfillment* (New York: Free Press, 2002).

———. *Flourish: A Visionary New Understanding of Happiness and Well-being* (New York: Free Press, 2011).

Martin Seligman, Nansook Park and Christopher Peterson, "Strengths of Character and Well-Being." *Journal of Social and Clinical Psychology*, Vol. 23, No. 5, (2004), 603–619.

William Shakespeare, *Hamlet* Act 1, Scene 3.

Daniel J. Siegel, *Mindsight* (New York: Bantam Books, 2010)

H. Siegel, *Relativism Refuted: A Critique of Contemporary Epistemological Relativism* (Dordrecht: D. Reidel, 1987).

Henry David Thoreau, *Walden* (Boston: Ticknor and Fields, 1854).

Hao Wang, *Reflections on Kurt Gödel* (Boston: MIT Press, 1987).

Alfred North Whitehead, *Process and Reality* (Free Press, 1979).

E. P. Wigner, "The Unreasonable Effectiveness of Mathematics in the Natural Sciences," in *Communications in Pure and Applied Mathematics*, vol. 13, No. I, (New York: John Wiley & Sons, 1960).

Oscar Wilde, *The Picture of Dorian Gray* (New York, Penguin Classics, 1890).

William Wordsworth, "Lines Written a Few Miles Above Tintern Abbey," printed in *Lyrical Ballads*, (London: J. & A. Arch, 1798).

Index

About the Author

Dr. William Cooney is a professor of philosophy at Hodges University and an adjunct professor at Florida Gulf Coast University in Southwest Florida. He earned his doctorate at Marquette University. He is past recipient of Teacher of the Year (Burlington Northern Faculty Excellence Award: Briar Cliff University) and Distinguished Scholarship Awards (Briar Cliff University and Marquette University).

His other books include *Reflections on Gabriel Marcel* (ed.), *Ten Great Thinkers*, *From Plato to Piaget*, and *The Quest for Meaning*. His articles appear in such professional journals as *Dialogue*, *Journal for Applied Ethics*, *The Encyclopedia of Applied Ethics*, and *The Encyclopedia of Death and Dying*.